10·11·79

THE COMPLETE CONDOMINIUM GUIDE

THE COMPLETE CONDOMINIUM GUIDE

by Bruce Cassiday

DODD, MEAD & COMPANY · NEW YORK

1 2 3 4 5 6 7 8 9 10

Library of Congress Cataloging in Publication Data

Cassiday, Bruce.
  The complete condominium guide.

  Bibliography: p.
  Includes index.
  1. House buying. 2. Condominium (Housing)
I. Title.
HD1379.C34   643   79–19312
ISBN 0–396–07725–0

Contents

2075373

1 • What a Condominium Is—and What It Isn't   1

2 • Boom and Bust and Boom Again   16

3 • The Shape of Today's Comdominium   34

4 • Comparison Shopping   49

5 • Checklist for Buyers   61

6 • Condo Traps—Beware!   73

7 • How to Finance a Mortgage   85

8 • Condominium Paper Chase   102

9 • Who Buys a Condo and Why—Is It for You?   117

10 • How the Management Structure Works   132

11 • Minigovernment: The Homeowners Association   148

12 • The Condominium *Is* the Future   159

     Bibliography   171

     Index   179

...1

What a Condominium Is--
and What It Isn't

MARGE HANSON and her husband, Bob, were having marital problems and had come to the point where they were about to break up. The trouble was that Marge had grown up in a small town and was used to the privacy of a home of her own and Bob had lived all his life in New York City and was used to the communal give-and-take of apartment house life.

The Manhattan apartment where they lived cost $350 a month and the rate was going up steadily. More or less as a desperation measure the Hansons bought a condominium in Connecticut. To the pleasant surprise of both of them, the town house into which they moved provided the answer to their separate—and combined—needs.

For Marge, it meant that she could putter around the place as much as she desired, could play tennis with friends on courts within condominium property bounds, and could do her own gardening in a small plot reserved especially for her on the grounds.

For Bob, it meant he could play cards when he wished with neighbors only two steps away, could read and watch television when he wanted rather than spend all his extra minutes patching up leaky roofs and repairing driveway cracks, and could even swim the whole year round in the condominium's enclosed pool.

Needless to say, Marge and Bob lived happily ever after.

A BLEND OF LIFESTYLES

Although it sounds like a real estate salesperson's dream, the story of Marge and Bob isn't at all an exaggerated or isolated one. The truth of the matter is that many people move into condominiums because they like the joy of private ownership and just as many do so because they like the fun of apartment life, where they don't have to contend with home maintenance chores.

Until several years ago people like the Hansons would have had no place to go to resolve their differences. You either rented a place in an apartment building or you bought a single-family house. What you rented belonged to your landlord, not to you. What you bought was your castle, pure and simple.

In the rented apartment you put up with noisy neighbors, failing heat, leaky faucets—unless you had a superior building superintendent. But you didn't have the responsibility of keeping the amenities in order. At the same time, all the improvements you made in the apartment— painting, repairs, and so on—weren't yours at all.

With the castle you bought went all its upkeep. When the shingles on the outside walls faded, you had to get out and paint them. When the plumbing went out of order, you had to fix it yourself or send for the plumber.

Within the past few years, however, the condominium, a new type of living arrangement, has appeared on the scene, offering an increasingly popular choice to any prospective homeowner/renter. Now, in a condominium, you can become in effect both renter *and* homeowner.

Briefly, the condominium offers a blend of individual and joint ownership. The word itself suggests joint dominium. *Condominium* comes from the Latin *dominium* ("ownership") and *con* is a combining form of *cum* ("with" or "together")—roughly, "ownership (shared) together with (others)."

ANATOMY OF A CONDOMINIUM

It works this way: You purchase the condominium—called "condo" for short—exactly like an individual house on a lot, except that you have full ownership rights only to the *inside* space of the house or apartment *as far as the walls.* You do not fully own the walls, floors, or ceiling!

You may also get exclusive use of a balcony, a patio, a garden space, and possibly a parking space. But, in addition, you share undivided ownership in the grounds around the structure, the exterior walls and hallways, lobbies, walks—everything *outside* your room space. You also share undivided ownership in all recreation facilities which come with the condominium.

THE CONCEPT OF REAL ESTATE

It may be necessary to back up a bit now in order to explain in some detail exactly how this novel concept of split ownership looks from a legal standpoint. Only when you understand that can you get an idea of the various advantages and disadvantages offered by the condominium.

Let's look first at real estate law. Most people think of real estate as a piece of ground marked off by stakes and property lines. Essentially, this view is absolutely correct. A parcel of property, called a "lot" in modern parlance, is located on the surface of the earth, bound by natural boundaries such as riverbanks and shore lines or artificial boundaries such as invisible lines from stake to stake. Once staked out, the parcel of property—real estate—is recorded in a land record office for future identification. It becomes an estate property that can be sold and bought.

The lines joining the stakes are not limited only to the plane of the earth's surface, but run upward to infinity and downward to the earth's core. All the property, not only on the earth's surface, but also that encompassed in all four vertical planes, represents the "estate in real property," separating it from all surrounding property.

Such a parcel of land can then be divided up into smaller plots of land, with each one an individual piece of property. Each plot of land, incidentally, is entirely inclusive of everything on that segment of the earth's surface. When you own a piece of "real estate," you own everything that lies upon it: the rocks, the trees, the streams, and anything erected by man, from tiny shacks to highrises.

For most people, this is as far as the concept of real estate goes. However, it is possible to look at real estate in another manner.

THE CONCEPT OF THE CONDOMINIUM

Let's suppose that a piece of real estate has a high-rise apartment building located on it and a small shack out back. You can see how easy it is to divide the property in two, with the shack on one piece of property and the high-rise on the other. Each piece becomes a viable segment of real estate.

It is also theoretically possible to divide the two-room

shack down the middle, where the rooms join, and the high-rise, say, according to the apartments on the ground floor. If we do divide the high-rise into rectangles that conform to the ground-floor apartments, each unit confined by its four vertical planes would then represent a separate parcel of property.

To take the matter one step further, it is obviously possible to divide the high-rise horizontally as well.

Then, with the vertical lines cutting through the apartment boundaries at the walls and confining one apartment to each segment and the horizontal lines cutting through the high-rise at every floor, we have what seems to be a pile of invisible cubes of air space inside the high-rise. The vertical planes are walls; the horizontal planes are floor and ceiling of each cube.

The division of a property into vertical and horizontal planes in this fashion is the essence of the condominium concept. Each condominium "cube" is called an "air space estate." All structural parts of the buildings land, and air space *outside* the various dwelling air space estates is property that is common to the owners of the dwelling units.

In the condominium concept, each owner of an air space estate also shares undivided ownership in all the common property of the larger condominium domain. This common area extends outwardly in all directions to the boundary lines of the original undivided condominium property. It is ownership of the common space that maintains the traditional real estate characteristics of the smaller units. If each living unit did not have an undivided interest in the common areas, like walls and floors, it would be suspended in space without orientation to anything and could not exist as a piece of real estate property.

The land upon which the high-rise is constructed is a

conventional piece of real estate. Its boundary lines *do* extend into the air to infinity and into the earth's core. The condominium concept has it that the owner of a dwelling unit in such a structure also has common undivided interest in all the rest of the structure and the sky, earth, and ground limited by the property lines. As such an owner, you must know where the boundaries of your condominium are in order to be sure where your undivided interest stops.

COMMON PROPERTY OF THE CONDOMINIUM

The common space in a condominium owned by all owners jointly is called by many different names—common area, common elements, common property, and common estate. For the purposes of this book, the common space will be called the "common property."

The cube of dwelling space each owner inhabits can be called individual unit estate, unit estate, unit dwelling, condominium unit, and so on. In this book the cube of dwelling space will be called the "condominium unit" or "living unit."

It is important to note that the space between the condominium units—that is, the walls, ceilings, and floors—and the roof and outer walls are all part of the condominium's common property. In addition, the grounds outside the structure all the way to the boundary lines, and the dirt and soil under the structure, as well as the sky above, are also part of the common property.

The legal description of this property must show the exact location of all structures on the land encompassed by the condominium property lines and the exact location and demarcation of each living unit within the condominium structure.

THE CONDOMINIUM'S "ENABLING DECLARATION"

The legal basis by which the condominium is created is called the "enabling declaration." This document is necessary in order to "enable" the condominium to come into being on the property in question. In fact, the condominium cannot exist until this declaration is recorded in the city clerk's office.

The declaration contains a description of the boundary lines of the total property, and also describes with detailed accuracy the various condominium units within the complex.

The importance of the enabling declaration cannot be overstressed. Since it must conform to all local and state regulations regarding condominiums, it is your guarantee that you are protected to the fullest extent of the law.

Besides the physical description of the common property and the individual condominium units, the declaration also contains the by-laws by which the condominium operates.

Provisions for professional management, hazard and liability insurance, replacement and operating reserves are usually included. Also, the undivided interest percentage —the ratio of a unit to the total of all the units—is established in the declaration.

The formula used to determine the undivided interest in the common property of the condominium affects each owner's percentage of ownership of the common property, the number of votes he controls in matters brought before the homeowners association, the amount of his assessment for maintenance and operation of the common properties, the amount of his undivided real estate assessment, and the amount of money a lender will be willing to loan on the unit and its percentage of common property.

Legally, the effect of this declaration is to convert a traditional single-deed estate into a multiple number of deeded dwelling unit estates within it. Each unit holder owns an undivided interest in the condominium's common property. In addition, each owner holds a separate deed of individual ownership to his own condominium unit.

Condominium ownership differs sharply from traditional real estate ownership. A condominium is actually created by a special real estate law that permits individual living units to be established within a total and larger property estate. Once the individual condominium units have been described within the total property estate, the remainder of the property—such as the grounds, the structural parts of the buildings, the common passageways—becomes a common estate.

The common property is then owned jointly by the owners of the individual condominium units. No condominium unit estate is complete without its undivided interest in the larger common estate.

Each owner is completely responsible for his own dwelling unit. He shares, with all the other owners, the common property. To maintain and keep up the common property the owners elect representatives called a board of directors, who in turn designate or hire a manager to maintain the entire condominium estate.

WHAT THE CONDOMINIUM CONCEPT MEANS TO YOU

The main consideration that makes the condominium a good financial investment is its relatively low cost. Undeveloped land near large cities and exciting recreational areas has become so much in demand, so crowded, and so expensive that it can no longer be used for the development of single-family houses on individual plots of ground. High-rise and multiple-unit structures—vertical or horizontal—can consolidate many living units to the acre and can also gain certain economies with large-scale construction. The result is that each unit costs far less than an individual structure of the same size would on the same piece of ground.

A second consideration that makes the condominium vital and important in today's recreation-minded society is the fact that there is almost no maintenance involved in keeping it up. To large segments of the population, particularly singles, young marrieds, and retirees, the freedom from responsibility for upkeep of private grounds is an advantage to be treasured.

As a third consideration, the condominium enables you to invest your money and make a profit by your investment. When you rent an apartment, you simply pay for rooms on a month-to-month basis. You put nothing away for the future—you build no equity in the property where you live. When you buy a condominium, you begin to build equity in the unit with each monthly mortgage payment you make, so that if you decide to move, you can sell your property, usually at a substantial gain. In fact, you may make enough in the transaction to pay the entire down payment on a new house.

The fourth plus feature of condominium living is the fact that no one can force you to move out at the end of a lease period as is possible when you rent an apartment. You *own* the condo unit until you decide to sell it, and you can sell it anytime you want.

Also, as the owner of property, you are eligible for a tax deduction on your income—not only for real estate tax purposes, but also for the interest paid on the mortgage. In the early years of ownership, interest on any mortgage makes up the bulk of your monthly payments.

Any increase in the value of the unit belongs to you. If you sell at a profit, your profit is a capital gain. Because it is a capital gain, you can defer the income tax payment if you buy another house. In fact, you can arrange the mortgage on a condominium unit in much the same way you do on a conventionally owned single house.

Within certain limitations, you can live in the unit, rent it, refinance it, sell it, or even bequeath it as you would any other piece of real property. All that—and recreation too!

Many condominiums make a point of providing recreational facilities right on the premises in the form of a swimming pool, tennis court, putting green, bowling alleys, and other facilities.

It's no wonder that the condo is rapidly becoming the new way of life for millions of Americans. It offers the best of two worlds—the better features of both home ownership and apartment renting.

THE LAST HOPE OF MIDDLE-CLASS HOUSING

"The dream of owning one's own home is fading more and more into the distance," says one observer of the housing scene. Expensive maintenance and energy costs are slowly putting the ownership of a house out of the reach of the average person.

The alternatives to home ownership are few, and most of them are discouraging. Rentals are becoming more expensive, are not tax deductible, and continually escalate. Cooperatives exist mainly in urban centers of the country —many are in New York City—and some people are apprehensive about owning shares of stock in a corporation rather than owning outright a deed to a property.

Condominium ownership gives the same tax advantages as owning a house and can in many ways be less expensive to maintain. A condominium often has the added benefit of many recreational extras.

According to one housing expert, the condominium has become "the last hope of middle-class housing." With prices of individual houses going through the inflation ceiling and making it impossible even for a family with two breadwinners to finance new homes, the condominium is the answer.

Basic economic factors favoring condominium ownership include the increasing number of people seeking housing—singles as well as couples—and rising single-family housing costs.

Instead there will be rising demand—especially in metropolitan areas—for various types of grouped, stacked, or clustered housing units that are economical and therefore attainable. These types of housing are the very ones which attract condominium ownership in practical price ranges.

THE COOPERATIVE—CITY COUSIN OF THE CONDOMINIUM

The condominium is actually a close cousin to an older and quite durable type of multiple residence—the cooperative. In fact, the two resemble each other as twins might, especially in their high-rise manifestation. But the co-op is still a city-bred sophisticate, and the condo is a wandering relative—a country cousin with a variety of guises not at all restricted to asphalt pavements.

As the owner of a co-op apartment, you do not hold a deed to your living unit. You own a share in a corporation, and the corporation owns the building.

Both co-op and condo are run by homeowners associations which elect a board of directors to manage the property. Both co-op and condo owners pay maintenance fees according to the size of their unit.

Generally speaking, the co-op is run on a tighter set of bylaws than the condo. Every co-op buyer must be approved by the co-op association. Not every condo demands such approval; in fact, most don't. A co-op owner, however, is frequently required to "help out" those who default on mortgage payments. A condo owner is required only to pay his own mortgage.

Ideal co-op and condo living both depend almost entirely on the skill of the board of directors and/or manager who runs the complex. A good board of directors makes for a happy co-op or condo. A "bad" board of directors— one that does not know how to run a tight ship and cannot afford to acquire a competent manager—will cause misery everywhere.

Results? Rapidly escalating maintenance fees. Sloppy upkeep. Rapid depreciation of property. Trouble all around.

PUD—THE CONDOMINIUM THAT ISN'T

The condominium has an interesting look-alike that might be a twin—but isn't even related! Actually, the co-op, the condo, and the look-alike were all spawned out of the same concept of living: controlled communality.

The condo's look-alike is called the planned unit development, or PUD. There is nothing *wrong* with the PUD —it is a viable way of life for many thousands of happy, contented people—but it is *not* a condominium, even though many people, some of whom live in PUDs, think it is.

The planned unit development, like the condominium, can take almost any form imaginable. Its advantage is its flexibility. The development can be elegant and expensive or simple and inexpensive. It can boast of many different types of recreational facilities or it can be devoid of them entirely.

It resembles a condominium in that it has a homeowners association, a board of directors that hires maintenance and upkeep personnel, and strict rules by which every member must abide, or be disciplined.

Nevertheless, the PUD is *not* a condominium. The unit owner in a PUD does not own an *undivided interest* in the common properties. The common properties are owned by a separate corporation or by the builder/developer himself.

Yet the unit owner must pay for the maintenance and upkeep of the common properties, including recreational areas, even though he does not hold interest in them. That is the difference which makes the PUD not a condominium.

Note: In some isolated instances, what resembles a PUD can be a legal condominium. The only way you can tell a true condominium is to determine by its enabling declaration or bylaws that all unit holders own undivided interest in the *entire property complex,* including roads and other areas.

THE NEW CONDOMINIUM LIFESTYLE

Today's increase in leisure time, the worldwide energy crisis, the population explosion that has forced people to live close together, the rebellion against the conformity and sterility of suburbia—all these factors have combined to make the more imaginative condominium ownership popular today.

In a way, the new condominium lifestyle is a revolution

in living habits that turns us back to the town meetings of Colonial times, to early-on "participatory democracy," to days when it was natural and necessary to work in close proximity to your neighbor—not only for the sake of cooperation, but for protection as well. Close contact with him not only gave one a sense of involvement and camaraderie, but a sense of personal respect and human values quite absent in today's essentially amoral world.

Certain observers have described the condominium as a Greek city-state in microcosm—a shelter within a village, a village within a city, a citadel free from urban blight. Carrying the analogy further, each condominium has a constitution by which the residents within its confines must abide, each has a vote on all issues in a one-man–one-vote apportionment.

The condominium is a self-policing, self-taxing, self-legislating body of people who live together in a political unit that is binding, that is practical, that is fulfilling, and that is psychologically satisfying.

Each time a condominium unit is sold out, new owners move in, the homeowners association changes, and the body politic is refined, shifted, and altered to a degree. A small republic comes of age. And it is then that the condominium owner is struck by the familiarity of the process and acts as if he has just discovered true democracy and citizenship.

Actually, it isn't quite that simple. The condo owner hasn't *discovered* democracy and citizenship. He's only rediscovered it. But he is making it work. In the process, the condominium owner has recovered the use and rediscovered the meaning of an almost forgotten, long-obsolescent word.

That word is *community.*

Long before this age of alienation, there was "community"—"communality," if you will—in all our lives. Welcome it back. It is alive and breathing in the new condominium lifestyle.

... 2

Boom and Bust and Boom Again

THERE is nothing new about the condominium as a living unit, even though many Americans had never heard the term until it came into vogue sometime during the 1960s.

The truth is that the condominium was a going thing as far back as 4,000 years ago! In fact, the earliest known record of a condominium has been traced to a Babylonian document estimated as originating about 2,000 B.C. This particular document recorded the sale of the first floor of a house, with the owner retaining title to the second floor.

In the Brooklyn Museum there is a papyrus dated 434 B.C. that describes a condominium apartment, annotates its boundaries, and contains specific instructions about the right of sale. It even mentions "title insurance."

CONDOMINIUMS ON THE TIBER

As the Roman Empire grew, desirable land, especially choice lots near the Forum, became extremely expensive and correspondingly scarce. The population squeeze led the Roman Senate to pass a law permitting Romans to own their own living units in multiunit buildings.

Retired Roman generals were often given an apartment—a condominium—in the city as reward for their service to the Empire.

Communal living continued in parts of Europe through the Middle Ages, when people who worked farms outside the city walls huddled together inside the walls at night for protection against the invading barbarians. Condominiums were a popular form of real estate inside these walled fortresses.

Early in the twentieth century, the condominium craze spread to Belgium, England, the Netherlands, France, Germany, Italy, and Spain—where statutes were enacted to permit them. When the condo crossed the Atlantic Ocean to Latin America—particularly in Brazil, Chile, Mexico, Puerto Rico, and Venezuela—it was called "horizontal property." Brazil passed horizontal property laws in 1928; Chile followed with similar legislation in 1937. In Venezuela, condominiums are now about the only type of house that most people can buy.

Even in 1947 there were a few condominiums in the United States, but there were no laws governing them. Puerto Rico, established as a free commonwealth by the United States in 1952, enacted condominium legislation in 1951, and did so again in 1958.

Crowded conditions on the congested island demanded some method of providing housing for low-income workers—of which the island had more than its share. Just like Rome, San Juan began sheltering its populace in small individually-owned cubes of living space, turning to its benefactor to the north for economic help in financing such arrangements.

The United States had never really become condominium-conscious. In Colonial America, the condominium concept made some inroads with settlers owning their own single homes individually and communally owning the commons—the large acreage in the center of town where their cattle grazed—exactly as the word *commons* implies: in common. But the current concept of the condominium did not appear in the United States until the 1960s. In 1961 the United States Congress included in Section 234 of the National Housing Act a clause to promote the building of condominiums for families in Puerto Rico. The clause was simply an extension of Federal Housing Administration insurance for mortgage loans.

ENTER "HORIZONTAL LIVING"

The act stimulated condominium construction, and within months dozens of them had sprung up in the congested areas of San Juan. Puerto Ricans moving into Miami and New York brought with them knowledge of the new lifestyle of "horizontal living"—the condominium.

Hawaii was the first state to adopt a condominium law. Enacted in 1961, it was called the "Horizontal Property Regimes Act." The Hawaii Act was based on Puerto Rico's law, but did not cover any contingencies other than the ability to create a condominium. It did not actually state any rights or obligations of condo buyers, sellers, or residents.

In 1962 the Federal Housing Administration drew up a condominium statute based on the Puerto Rican laws that has since served as a model for states enacting their own laws. Between 1962 and 1968 the idea of the condominium spread rapidly throughout the United States, with scores of new high-rises units built to be sold rather than rented. Most state legislatures began passing laws to enable lending institutions to make loans for the financing of condominium ownership.

And so the boom began.

THE BIG CONDOMINIUM BOOM

By 1969, fifty condominiums had been completed in New York and Michigan. Chicago had over 7,000 units within its environs. When Miami was authorized to build and sell condominium apartments by the Florida legislature in 1964, the flood gates were open.

The result was the nucleus in Miami of the condominium craze. Communal life had always been an attraction for retired couples. And Miami had always been their mecca.

When Miami was opened up to condominiums, tens of thousands of retired Americans migrated south to become condominium owners. What resulted was, unfortunately, not paradise, as hinted at in the attractive sales brochures that promised every condominium owner a carefree place in the sun, but something almost the opposite of paradise. At best, the condominium boom was chaos.

By 1970, there were 85,000 condo units in the United States. In the first half of 1972, 38,000 housing permits for condominiums were registered in the Miami–Fort Lauderdale area. In the state of Florida itself there were 146,000 building permits issued for condominium construction.

Figures show that in 1973 there were approximately 350,000 condominium starts recorded in the United States. It was a record to that date—and, ironically enough, a record that has not yet been equaled in the years since.

The market was still humming in 1974. A survey made in that year by the Department of Housing and Urban Development estimated optimistically that half the population of the country would be living in condominiums by 1994. In 1974 alone, condominiums constituted 14.3 percent of the total housing constructed, compared to only 8 percent in 1972.

Like most runaway successes, the condo boom brought all sorts of developers and real estate entrepreneurs out into the open to cash in on the bonanza. For every well-built and honestly advertised condominium, there were others put up with poor design and shoddy construction.

How to Wreck a Living Unit

Builders who were trying to squeeze everything they could out of every dollar cut as many corners as they could. Some substitutions were legitimate—others were not.

One Florida contractor connected ocean water to the air-conditioning system of a building, apparently not realizing the water was brine and not pure water. The salt water corroded the system beyond repair after its first year of operation. The entire unit was ruined. The condominium owners had to pay $5,000 apiece to replace it. Another builder substituted galvanized water pipes for brass. Within two years, the entire plumbing system had to be ripped out to the walls and replaced at the owners' expense.

Shoddy construction was only part of the chaotic situation. Ambivalent clauses buried in complicated contracts cost owners more than they had bargained for. Some developers inserted stipulations in sales contracts that gave them the right to run the condominium complex as they saw fit even after all the units were sold, contrary to condominium practice. Since the management fee was a fixed percentage of the project's total cost and maintenance, the developer was never too concerned about keeping within the maintenance budget when he operated the complex.

Many developers promised to provide management until the entire complex was completed and all units sold. There was so much money to be made quickly that they were very little concerned about *completing* the complex. One developer in Florida started a project which would "eventually" include eleven different two-building complexes. After several years, buyers began wondering: "Our management contract runs for fifteen years after the *last* building is complete. When is that going to be?"

At one Florida condominium managed by the developer, the condominium owners association paid the developer $60,000 a year *not* to manage the project. The owners found that it was a lot less expensive to manage the complex themselves. They wound up paying the developer's attorney $10,000 a year, even though they had no need for his services.

TROUBLE IN THE SUN COUNTRY

The boom brought its share of horror stories. In many cases monthly payments for upkeep and repairs turned out to be two or three times what the salespeople had estimated. There were instances of swimming pools, tennis courts, and other recreational amenities that were promised but never built. In other cases heavy monthly payments went to developers for "rental cost" of a swimming pool or other service that might not even have been built.

At one expensive condominium the residents were asked to pay $3,000 apiece for parking spaces. At one 502-unit high-rise in Miami Beach, the developer retained the title to the land on which a lavish swimming pool was built, charging the residents $311,352 a year for "land rent" on a ninety-nine-year contract. Ironically enough, the land on which the facility was built was as sessed for tax purposes at $82,000.

Residents of a posh complex in North Miami had to pay $221,000 for the use of its recreational facilities. And there was a cost-of-living clause written into the contract that pushed the total up even further than that year after year!

All the trouble was not confined to Florida. In Califor nia, after twenty-nine purchasers had taken title to their units in one condominium complex, the developer sud denly withdrew the remaining unsold units of the com plex and changed the development into a low-priced month-to-month rental complex. As a result, each of the twenty-nine owners found that his $20,000 investment was worth $5,000 or less.

THE VERY SMALL PRINT

Many of the problems arose from legal technicalities in the very complicated and finely printed condominium contracts. Most were long and contained more than their share of legalese, becoming utterly incomprehensible to the average homeowner.

In several instances even retired lawyers signed ency clopedic documents with barely a glance at the fine print. Later, when they took occupancy, they learned to their chagrin that their financial obligations were larger and their ownership rights less clearly defined than they had been led to believe. It was difficult to prove deception inasmuch as everything was spelled out on paper in the contracts.

Most of the abuses centered around two practices: the so-called "recreational lease" and gimmicks in the "man agement contract."

THE NINETY-NINE-YEAR RECREATIONAL LEASE

The "recreational lease" problem grew out of a custom dating back to the first days of condominium development in Florida. The builder would advertise the condominium units in such a way that the prospective owner thought he would have free use of *all* recreational facilities within the condominium's boundaries.

In actual practice, the builder might hold title to the area in which the swimming pool was located. Then, once the condominium owners took over the management of the project from him, he would lease the swimming pool back to the buyers for ninety-nine years. In some cases the lease contract had an escalating clause tied to the cost of living that made the yearly cost rise as inflation continued. The fees became astronomical after a time. Early builders claimed that they should be able to reap some profit from their successes in developing and selling the condominium; they felt that by charging for the use of the pool they were making an honest profit.

Eventually the "recreational lease" as such became outlawed by the courts. Many salespeople, it was found, would inform the condominium buyer verbally that he would be entitled to "free" use of all project facilities: the pool, the tennis courts, the club rooms, and anything else within the condominium boundaries. However, in the wording of the contract itself one or more of these facilities would be withheld, with each unit owner obligated to pay a fee for its use or face the threat of foreclosure action. Or the facility would be leased back to the owners of the condominium by the builder.

In a variation of the ploy the buyer would agree to pay a small fee for the use of a certain facility or facilities. Then, later, after reading the entire contract through, he would realize that he was paying the builder for something that the builder did not have any right to!

Recreational lease cases clogged the courts. In one of them the owners at a North Miami Beach condominium were entitled by their contract to free use of *all* recreational amenities—but with one important exception, as they were to discover. That exception was the swimming pool and surrounding deck, for which they were required to pay a use fee. The pool was so small that a maximum of nine swimmers were permitted in it and on the deck at one time. Yet the developer collected $19,620 a month from the 652 owners for that "privilege" alone!

Management Contract Gimmicks

As for the myriad of tricks concealed in "management contracts," they were many and varied. One family arrived in Florida to take over a condominium apartment it had purchased only to find another family already living in it. After a great deal of controversy, lawyers found that the second family was actually the legal owner. The contract had a trick clause. The clause allowed the management to seize any apartment and resell it if the owner of the unit failed to pay a $60 monthly recreation fee for the complex's swimming pool. The original owners were under the not-so-strange assumption that they didn't have to pay the fee until they were living in the complex and actually able to use the pool. They were wrong. In the end, they were forced to forfeit the entire $30,000 they'd originally paid for the unit! They wound up suing the owner.

While buyers were tearing their hair out over inequities, and sellers were promising to do better, apartment building operators suddenly discovered an ingenious way to unburden themselves of unprofitable buildings and get in on the condominium boom at the same time.

A NEW WRINKLE: CONVERSION

Saddled for years with escalating costs and unable to pass them on to their tenants, apartment owners saw the condominium craze as a good way out of their financial straits. Instead of continuing to rent apartment units, they began to "convert" a vacancy as soon as it occurred into a condominium—*sell* it rather than rent it.

Still, buying pressure did not slacken. When landlords had no vacancies to convert to condominiums, they found a way to create them. It was a simple matter to raise the rents too high for their tenants to pay, and evict them when their leases ran out.

Converted condominiums displaced a large number of tenants who could not afford to buy and were forced out of their homes. Conversions caused large blocs of rental housing to become suddenly unavailable to people with only moderate incomes, to people who were living on fixed incomes, and to young people who were just getting started. Older people on fixed incomes were bearing the brunt: they didn't have the money to buy what they rented. Many were forced out of apartments perhaps after living twenty-five years in them. Many were given thirty days to leave.

HUD RIDES TO THE RESCUE

By the early 1970s, it had become quite apparent that condominium buyers, who were flocking to the courts and clamoring for justice, needed some help from the government.

The Department of Housing and Urban Development held a series of hearings in 1973 and 1974. These hearings in turn instigated the first national survey ever made on the condominium situation. The findings of the survey were released by government officials in 1975, after which the Federal Trade Commission decided that consumer protection was needed in the field of condominium construction.

Nevertheless, the upshot of all this activity was that HUD finally decided that there were not actually enough widespread abuses sufficient to justify federal regulation beyond the normal safeguards applying to FHA-financed projects and that any special consumer protection necessary should come from the states. This finding spurred the states to action. Most passed condominium laws.

Hawaii passed a series of laws designed to protect the condominium buyer. Virginia passed a statute in 1974 that required various advance disclosures by developers, mandated a cooling-off period for buyers, and provided for two-year warranties against structural defects.

Florida and Georgia set up condominium regulatory agencies in 1975. Maryland and the District of Columbia passed ordinances controlling the conversion of rental properties into condominiums, as did Massachusetts, which also specified advance disclosure information. So did New York State. One of New York's most important laws concerned conversion of apartments from rental properties to condominiums. The legislation forbade conversions without 35 percent approval of all the tenants in the building. Tenants generally resisted conversion in those days, because they feared exchanging a stable rent —some of the apartments were still under rent control— for maintenance charges that would rise with increased building operating expenses.

Between 1974 and 1975 condominiums accounted for over 25 percent of all residential housing starts in the United States. The speed of condominium starts was picking up rapidly. In 1975 the rate came to almost 40,000 starts. By April 1975 there were a total of 1.25 million condo units in the United States.

Nor did developer abuses dry up. Agitation by condominium owners for legislation to protect them continued. But condo owners were not about to get satisfaction for their grievances. A shift in the economy trapped them in a sudden backwash of inactivity.

What happened was that the real estate market suddenly developed a shortage of breath. Prices retreated. Offerings failed to move. The housing market stagnated. In 1975 the rate of sales abruptly lagged. By April only 44 percent of the 40,000 units had been purchased, and by the end of the year only 68 percent.

THE BUST AFTER THE BIG BOOM

The depressed real estate market of 1974 caused condominium activity to cease abruptly. Condominium builders considered themselves lucky even to find buyers. Sellers were happy to get out of their condominium units with the money they had put into them.

By 1975 there was a glut of condominiums up for sale. Against this background state legislatures were able to pass strict laws that put a halt to much of the shaky financial manipulations that had been haunting condominium construction.

"We needed those laws," one condominium dealer said. "Even if they did put a lot of developers out of business. We had to improve the level of professionalism in the field, provide breathing space and allow for pressure to build up again and confidence to return."

With the condominium market depressed and state legislatures across the country passing more stringent laws to protect buyers against fly-by-night builders, there was a lag in condominium activity, and it looked for a while as if the condo bubble had burst. Construction on communal living units ground to a halt.

However, another factor was at work which eventually proved very promising for an upsurge in the condominium market: inflation. The price of single-family homes had begun pushing up because of excessive demand for housing spurred on by easily available money. In urban and suburban areas particularly, the rise was phenomenal. Inflation was at work on rental properties, too, with landlords passing on the higher costs in higher rents.

Empty condominiums began filling up; their price, even though inflated, was well below the general average of single-family houses. In 1976, there were 82,000 condo starts, but builder optimism proved to be as inflated as the economy. At least 15,000 of these condos became reverse conversions from condo to rental units, reducing the net total of condos finished to 40,000 at most.

However . . .

AND BOOM AGAIN!

A sudden new wave of buyers began flooding the market, picking up all the empty units available, and forcing up the price on occupied units. The buyers' market of the bust years became a sellers' market in the boom years.

Even those condo developments that had gained an initially bad image because of management problems were cleaning up their act by restructuring their management boards and evolving workable maintenance programs. Condos once again became desirable buys.

As the condominium image improved, real estate agents who had formerly avoided condominium sales because of buyer uneasiness realized their reputations would no longer be tarnished by encouraging the purchase of condos. They began to recommend them as a viable alternative to the overpriced single-family dwelling.

At the same time, an increase in the number of potential buyers made the condominium a hot market item. More singles, recently divorced parents, young career couples, and empty nesters—unable to procure single-unit houses—began coming into the condo market. It was a natural one for them.

Before builders could jump in and begin constructing new complexes, condo units were suddenly exhausted. Potential buyers hounded owners to sell; prices skyrocketed. With new building units projected but not yet ready for occupancy, dealers turned once again to older buildings that were losing money in rentals and began converting them to condominiums. The advantage was obvious: the sellers would have unprofitable buildings off their hands and money in their pockets.

NEW YORK STATE PASSES A LAW

New York and Washington, D.C., were affected heavily by these legal but unfortunate "conversions." New York State finally passed a cooperative-conversion law in Albany on July 27, 1978. Applying to Westchester, Nassau, and Rockland Counties, the law set up guidelines for turning rental apartments into ownership apartments.

The statute was intended to insure that all tenants be fully informed when a conversion was being proposed, that a significant number of the tenants wanted it, and that those who did not want to buy their apartments—or could not—be protected from harassment.

Tenants who chose to convert would have a choice of two plans: one allowing for eviction and the other barring it. If the tenant who decided not to purchase was to be evicted, the conversion would have to be approved by 35 percent of the tenants in the apartment, and no evictions would be allowed for two years.

If the converting tenants chose not to evict the nonpurchasing tenants, the consent of only 15 percent of the tenants would be needed. Tenants who wished to convert would have a year to get the necessary approval; if they failed, they would be unable to try again for another eighteen months. Under no circumstances could anyone over the age of sixty-two years be evicted, except for breach of lease.

The bill also was intended to insure that the same building services be offered in a "nondiscriminatory fashion" to all tenants—whether they bought their apartments or not—while the conversion was taking place.

Condominium production for 1977 was approximately 200,000, reflecting the gathering surge of housing activity. Of these, some 100,000 were multifamily condominiums, at least 50,000 single-family units, and about 50,000 conversions from rental to condo.

One-third of these were in California, and almost one-fifth in Florida. Chicago, Houston, and Washington all accounted for several thousand units. Conversions were heavy in Chicago and Houston, and strong in Los Angeles, San Diego, and Washington. By the end of 1977, government figures showed that over 4,000,000 Americans were living in just slightly fewer than 2,000,000 condominiums. A report in *Business Week* in October 1977 stated that condominiums accounted for 18 percent of all nonsubsidized apartments being built in the United States.

Chicago and San Francisco passed more stringent regulations covering conversions, and by early 1978 escalating costs of construction and conversion of apartments to condominiums had caused the national vacancy rate of apartment buildings to drop to 5.1 percent—the lowest rate in twenty-four years. In addition, 75,000 units were absorbed from unsold condos languishing on the market. The visible inventory of long unsold units, over 200,000 in 1975, decreased to less than 50,000.

In the once heavily overbuilt Miami–Fort Lauderdale market, the inventory dwindled from 30,000 units in 1975 to under 12,000. Only some 3,000 condos remained for sale in Washington, D.C., where there had been as many as 20,000.

LOOKING AHEAD THROUGH ROSE-COLORED GLASSES

After a great deal of backing and filling, the condominium market began a strong upsurge once again during the last weeks of 1978. Conversions still involved a large percentage of "new" condo units. The total of condominium starts for 1978 was close to 300,000, almost matching the record 350,000 of 1973. Condominiums made up the strongest sector of the housing market—quite a turnaround from the low point in 1975.

In Chicago, the condominium market was booming, creating a housing crunch on Chicago's North Side, drying up the rental market, forcing rents up nearly 50 percent in some of the best areas of the city and suburbs. Nearby, in suburban Evanston, condo conversions reduced the apartment vacancy rate to less than one percent, pushing up rent increases as high as 60 percent in some buildings. One in ten of Evanston's rental units have so far been converted to condominiums.

In Boston, most condominium conversions were selling out within three to twelve months, with waterfront units going for $100,000 to $200,000 and city units $30,000 to $50,000.

In Washington, D.C., condominium sales hit 10,000 in 1978, with about 2,000 units that year converted from rentals to condos.

In New York, only 5 percent of the city's housing inventory were condominiums in 1978. But in the suburbs, condominiums accounted for at least half of the for-sale multifamily housing.

In Atlanta, the condominium inventory was down 1,500 in 1978 from 8,000 in 1977.

In the Dallas–Fort Worth area, new condominium units were being built at a rate of 2,000 a year. Garden apartments were being converted to condominiums within the $25,000 to $50,000 price range.

In Houston, condominiums priced between $30,000 to $50,000 were selling well on the city's west side.

The Miami–Fort Lauderdale area saw their condominium inventory down to about 8,000 in 1978, with sales strong in the semiluxury and luxury models—$85,000 to $600,000.

In Denver, conversions were going very strongly, with about 4,000 in 1978. Typically, a new 120-unit building, with units from $70,000 to $120,000, was two-thirds sold out before construction began.

In Los Angeles, condominiums and town houses in 1978 made up half the for-sale market, in the $40,000 to $90,-000 range. Conversions along Wilshire Boulevard were waiting for city approval; these were selling at from $125 to $140 a square foot. One Beverly Hills builder was selling million-dollar condos!

In San Diego, condominiums and town houses accounted for 40 percent of the for-sale market, with conversions making up about 25 percent of the condo stock. Most new condos in the $80,000 range pulled five inquiries per unit.

In the San Francisco–Oakland area, conversions from rentals to condominiums were selling out quickly, particularly in southern locations. One 230-unit conversion was two-thirds sold out in four months.

In Seattle, condominium sales and conversions were catching up and growing steadily in 1978—particularly in the low to medium price ranges.

Obviously, the condominium owner does not seem to have any need to fear that the value of his well-located condominium will depreciate. Nevertheless, as a potential buyer, you are advised to read and understand every provision in the sales contract before you sign.

...3

The Shape of Today's Condominiun

ALTHOUGH the condominium concept was originally developed in its contemporary sense exclusively in high-rise residential apartment buildings, it soon came to be applied to duplexes, garden apartments, town houses, single-unit resort homes, and even commercial office space.

Condominiums resolve themselves into two broad major categories: residential and commercial.

In turn, residential condominiums break down into three types: urban, suburban, and resort.

THE RESIDENTIAL CONDOMINIUM

The most popular and recognizable type of condominium property today is the residential living unit. Residential condominiums in the early years of condominium popularity were usually apartment units in high-rise buildings close to or within the country's large urban centers.

Today many other types of residential condominium units are available in the suburban areas surrounding metropolitan centers as well as in the middle of the cities. All these types are basically similar and can be categorized as "urban condominiums."

THE URBAN CONDOMINIUM

Within the metro areas, most condominium residences tend to be limited to high-rise buildings. These condominium units are either in the form of brand-new construction or of older apartment buildings that have been converted from rental units to condominium units.

In certain sections, usually farther out from the center of the city, "mid-rise" buildings of from three to five stories serve as condominium complexes. There are even "low-rise" complexes as well—one or two stories in height. Nevertheless, the high-rise is still the predominant and most conspicuous type of condominium structure in and around urban centers.

Some urban condominium complexes include street-level stores and shops within the confines of the condominium proper. These are owned and operated jointly by the condominium unit owners through their condominium association and are rented out or leased to retailers and store managers to bring in rental fees to help defray condominium maintenance costs.

In some projects, these street-level store spaces are sold to retailers as commercial condominiums. The retailer then becomes a condominium unit owner, and as such is entitled to membership in the homeowners association, with the power to vote on any actions taken. Some states have laws forbidding this practice; others allow it.

The office space may even be retained by the developer himself to be used in any way he may devise for income purposes. It all depends upon the condominium rules and regulations. 2075373

Why Live in an Urban Condo? The big-city condominium has created a brand-new lifestyle for many thousands of people who at one time lived in rented city apartments. Condominium owners fall into two general categories of people. First, there is the group of young married couples who seek the advantages of home ownership but who unfortunately are unable to afford the highly inflated prices of suburban single-family homes. Second, there is another group of city dwellers who would never give up the conveniences and the ambiance of the city but who want to benefit by the tax shelters they can get from direct ownership and cannot get from renting.

It is a new opportunity for these two groups to enjoy the advantages of big-city life and at the same time fight inflation through appreciating property values, building equity in fully owned property, and taking advantage of the IRS's deductions for real estate tax payments and mortgage interest.

Condominium ownership has added another intangible value to their lives. Because they own their living units, most of them feel a companionship with their neighbors, who also are homeowners, rather than the typical off-handed attitude one transient renter has for another.

Psychologically, an owner of a property feels greater kinship with it than the renter of a property. Because condo dwellers are owners, they tend to take more interest in keeping their property up, creating a more favorable living environment for themselves and their neighbors.

Condominium ownership creates such big-city oddities as organized work parties to clean up common property, social get-togethers, and cooperation with one another on all levels of living unheard of ordinarily in rented apartments.

The condo owner *wants* to remodel his apartment. When he does a good job on it, he is not only raising the value of his unit but improving the image of the entire building by enhancing the whole. A condo owner wants quality maintenance and upkeep so as not to sustain a loss in his property values. If the property degenerates, he will not be able to sell it for as much as he would if it improved in quality.

Even though as an owner he must deal with rising taxes and maintenance fees—which a landlord had to cope with before—he has effectively eliminated the landlord's profit and spiraling rents.

The city condominium also offers a welcome alternative for the suburban homeowner who wants the cultural advantages and dynamism of city living. In some cases couples whose children have grown up unload their suburban homes, which are now nothing more than big, rattling, almost empty nests, and move back into the city as condo owners to become involved in activities and recreation while still enjoying the benefits (both psychological and financial) of home ownership.

THE SUBURBAN CONDOMINIUM

Spread throughout the areas surrounding the large metro centers are numerous types of condominium complexes. Some of these appear in the form of high-rise buildings, but more generally the suburban form tends to run to the garden apartment, cluster housing units, town houses, duplexes, "fourplexes," mansion units, and even so-called "country estates."

The *garden apartment* usually takes the form of a small group of "mid-rise" buildings—some "low-rise" two-story structures and others as high as perhaps five stories—placed in an area that is carefully and imaginatively landscaped.

The "common green," which the grounds are called, lends an ambiance to the area, affording the owners a place to walk and sit outside—and all within the confines of the complex. Naturally, every condominium unit owner has a common undivided interest in the grounds within the boundary lines of the property.

The *cluster housing unit* usually takes the form of a group of multiunit structures, each housing from two to four condominium units apiece. Each of these units has its own private entranceway. Cluster housing can appear as duplexes, triplexes, "fourplexes" and so on, or it can be a cluster of small multiunits around a larger mid-rise multiunit.

These cluster units occupy well-landscaped, self-confining grounds that provide areas for walking, exercising, recreation, and general lounging about.

The *town house* is an extremely popular type of condominium design which has been springing up in all parts of the country. The old meaning of town house usually referred to individual homes built side by side with common walls in a manner reminiscent of urban scenes from the nineteenth century. These row houses might be landscaped by grounds both in front and in back, with the entire block set off by artistically placed trees and shrubs.

Many modern condominium town houses are of this type, especially in the more established parts of cities—particularly those which have been converted to condominiums from rental duplexes.

However, at the present time, the term town house has come to mean not only attached row houses, but semi-attached houses in rows and not in rows, and in some cases, even detached houses. In fact, the fastest-proliferating type of town house today is the "country town house" —a complete contradiction in terms if there ever was one.

One such "country town house" complex in fact has advertised itself as initiating "numerous departures from the ordinary condominium format" to "render them homes, not apartments." The purport of the ad is of course to make it clear that the "country town house condominium" is *not* an apartment-type high-rise condominium.

Such a complex resembles a more elaborate type of planned unit development—except that it is a true condominium in the sense that each unit owner holds undivided interest in the complex's common property.

As is obvious, the so-called town house unit can be quite elaborate, or it can be quite inexpensive, depending on its design, its construction, its location, and its general appearance.

The *duplex,* or double, is a relative newcomer to the condominium scene. In appearance it resembles a large single-family home. The grounds are in no way elaborate. It is simply a condominium house in which two condo units co-exist as one, with each owner sharing joint, undivided interest in the common area.

The *fourplex,* or quadruplex, is another newcomer to the condominium scene. It appears to be a rather large, old-fashioned, New England type of house. Instead of two separate living units, it has four—each with its own entry and exit.

There is even a "triplex," and perhaps, a "fiveplex," but as can be seen the terms become endless, and obvious.

The *mansion unit* is another brand-new innovation in condominiums. Many such mansions were built in the nineteenth century in America during a time when families were large and servants were many. The type of house described in *Gone With the Wind* is typical of the size and style of such a mansion.

Many of these old homes have been refurbished and split up into various separate living units—each a kind of suite in itself. Some old mansions divide into six units, some into fewer, and others into more. The difference between the mansion unit and the fourplex is that the mansion unit owner enters and exits through a common front door.

The living unit is a special suite of rooms within the mansion wholly owned by the unit owner. The common property includes the stairways, the entryways, and perhaps the central reception area in the front of the house. There are many different ways to split up an old mansion.

The *country estate* goes one step further than the mansion unit. This type of condominium project is a more elegant and expensive version of the cluster housing unit —an elaborate alternative for the affluent homeowner who doesn't want to saddle himself with the woes of upkeep and maintenance but who wants a noble-looking manse and does not want to be confined to the smaller condominium units of conventional design.

The estate house condo unit may be in the form of a single-unit house or a multiple dwelling with separate condominium units in it. The landscaping is usually lush, with large areas of green surrounding the living unit. In appearance, the country estate resembles the type of dwelling familiar to the English countryside during the Edwardian days: separate structures representing the carriage house, the servants' quarters, the caretaker's cottage, and the manse itself.

Such an estate might even contain some esoteric recreational facilities of real splendor. These might include screening rooms, gambling tables, sauna baths, swimming pools, tennis courts, squash courts, game rooms, bridle paths, cinder paths, and so on. The grandeur of the country estate condominium is virtually limitless.

Still in the formation stage, the country estate may even

be an actual country estate built in the last century that has become too expensive to manage and has been converted to condominium units. In condominium fashion, each unit owner holds deed to his own unit privately, owns individual interest in all common property, and shares in the common fees charged for running the entire country estate.

In the more imaginative developments, the condo complex can offer someone of unlimited resources a completely new way of life. Each condominium owner can have whatever convenience he is capable of paying for. Such conveniences might include a common shopping center, a restaurant or café, a moving picture theater, a music hall, entertainment and recreational facilities of all kinds, and even health-care facilities for older persons.

Many condominium communities have been developed for different kinds of people: singles, retirees, young marrieds, sportsmen, artists and writers, joggers, golfers, sailors, and so on.

At the other end of the scale, some more simple suburban residential condominiums may be nothing more than a series of single-family attached homes, all utilizing the same common land and parking areas, with each unit self-contained and isolated from the others—but sometimes only thinly. Each, of course, owns an undivided interest in all common properties for which he pays maintenance and upkeep through an association of all owners.

Why Live in a Suburban Condo? The suburban condominium offers a life free from the responsibilities of home maintenance—one of the most negative features of home ownership for many people—and adds an even more attractive advantage by providing recreational facilities such as swimming pools, tennis courts, and sauna baths.

In addition, the suburban condo owner usually has excellent security service provided in the condominium during his absence. Because the cost of these services is shared by all owners, it can be kept within reason.

The suburban condo generally appeals to one of three kinds of people:

First, there is the homeowner who has decided that he was being cheated out of his leisure time by always being on call to paint the house, mend the fence, weatherstrip the doors and windows, and put in the storm windows. Maintanence-free life appeals to him.

Secondly, there is the older person who wants to break away from the bedeviling experience of repairing his home and some of the heavier chores that he can no longer handle easily physically. Community activities around the condominium complex are attractive lures to him as well.

Third, there is the suburbanite who likes suburbia but has rented apartment units all his life because of an inability to pay the huge sums needed to buy a private single-family home. The suburban condo, usually more modestly priced than a single-family home, is the answer to his desire to live in the suburbs and to reap the advantages of home ownership without being subjected to rising rents.

THE RESORT CONDOMINIUM

Up to this point we have been talking about condominium units that are used as a principal place of residence. Now let's look at an entirely different kind—a second-home type of condominium that has made a considerable place for itself in the sun.

With the increase in leisure time afforded every American by technological advances in industry and the more humane approach of the corporate entity to its employees, it was only natural that condominium development should have grown quickly in resort areas.

It is now not uncommon to find condominiums in ski country, in lake country, on the sea coast, at the marina, near the golf course, and even in the outreaches of hunting and backpacking country. In warmer areas of the country, where the sun resorts are located, condominium complexes can be found grouped around the common recreational facility for which the area is famed.

In form, the resort condominium itself can range from individual houses and cluster units right on up to high-rise towers. Some units may even appear in the form of modular housing, constructed in standardized units placed together to form different configurations of multiunit structures. Some may be in the form of simple cluster housing as well.

Resort condominiums provide skiing and skating in the winter and tennis, swimming, golf, horseback riding, and sailing in the summer.

Resort condominium units may differ from the residential condos in more than appearance. Some living units may be owned jointly with several other people. This concept is called "time sharing" and is a fairly new living mode that has burgeoned among the recreation-minded set.

Time Sharing and How It Works. "Time sharing" began in Europe in the 1960s among recreation-minded world travelers who chose to ski in the Alps in the winter and sail boats on the Mediterranean in the summer. It is also called "interval ownership," "vacation ownership," or "villa shares."

Very simply, "time sharing" is time-interval ownership in a condominium unit located at or near a resort area.

What you buy is not the condominium unit per se, but a *piece* of the unit for use during a certain part of the year.

It's an idea that has grown rapidly in the past few years. Today thousands of Europeans own time shares in chalets in the Alps and beach condominiums on the Mediterranean. And many Americans now own time shares from Hawaii to Puerto Rico, from Florida to Washington State, in everything from small campsites to elaborate high-rise complexes.

Many resorts include tennis courts, swimming pools, and other recreational facilities in addition to the regular feature of the resort. Some offer golf and boating. Others have special rates for nearby golf courses and marinas.

It works like this. You purchase a particular condominium unit for two weeks of each year. That means that you have a 1/26 ownership in the condominium unit. However, instead of paying, say, $100,000 for the condominium unit, you pay somewhere between $3,000 to $6,000 for the interval. The average weekly price for a resort condo is somewhere between $1,000 and $3,000.

In addition to the purchase price of the time-shared condominium unit, you have to pay annual expenses which come to anywhere between $100 to $200 a week. However, that's better than the $1,000 or $3,000 you'd have to pay if you owned it for fifty-two weeks of the year.

With all these costs in mind, it is important to remember that the daily tariff for a condominium unit is generally far less per person than the cost of comparable accommodations at a quality resort hotel. And with the condo you don't have to go through the hassle of securing rooms in advance.

In addition, you have the privilege of a kitchen and living room, and possibly a terrace or patio. If you have children, your expenses will be cut considerably with the added use of the kitchen at your disposal.

Financing isn't hard. Most time-sharing units can be bought with 10 to 25 percent down, and the balance payable over five years or so. Your time-share interest can be sold or used as collateral. If the property is maintained and the resort area continues to flourish, the chances are good that your time share will increase in value.

You are less likely to be subject to vandals and burglars in a time-shared condo unit than you would be in your own place, with it unoccupied a great deal of the time.

Purchase of a share of time in a resort condominium unit is a good hedge against vacation inflation. Your living unit is also salable, as any condo unit is. Whatever profit you make on purchase and sale is a capital gain. But you can deduct the real estate tax you pay on the condominium unit and also the interest on a loan if you take one out to buy the unit.

You can usually buy time segments from one to thirteen weeks. The amount you pay varies according to the size and location of the resort and whether you take it at an in- or off-season time.

Most such condominium units include maid service and give you a change of linen once a week. External maintenance is also provided. You do not need to belong to the homeowners association.

In addition, many time-share resorts in the United States belong to exchange networks, also called reciprocal-use agencies. Through these, you can swap your two weeks at one resort for two weeks at another resort. Member resorts may include those in Spain, Mexico, Canada, the Caribbean Islands, and sites all over the United States.

Of course, the beauty of the resort condominium is its tremendous adaptability. If you want to, you can use it as a year-round residential unit, or you can use it as a part-time residential unit, renting it out to someone else either during the off-season or on-season months.

Who Wants a Resort Condominium? The resort condominium has a widespread appeal, not only for the suburban homeowner who uses the unit with his family on weekends and rents it to his friends during the week but also for the investor who owns his unit and rents it out the year round for money-making purposes.

The owner who does not use the condo at all but rents it out not only receives an income to help offset the expenses before taxes, but he also receives additional deductions on his income tax for real estate taxes and mortgage interest.

Potentially, the resort condo is a good investment for anyone—even for one who does not avail himself of the recreational facilities but simply uses the purchase for rental income.

THE COMMERCIAL CONDOMINIUM

Geared to the professional, the businessman, or a business concern, the *commercial condominium* is simply office space that is owned rather than rented.

Like any condominium concept, the owner has control over his particular office space and shares an undivided interest with other owners in the common elements of the building or buildings of the condominium. He pays taxes and mortgage only on his condominium unit, and pays his own maintenance fee for upkeep of the building in proportion to the size of his own unit.

Usually the commercial condominium is limited to smaller office buildings in which each owner has space of his own for his business or occupation.

Frequently dentists and doctors own adjacent units and share such common property as laboratory and reception areas. Lawyers sometimes share condominium complexes in which each lawyer or law firm has a particular office space. Other professionals, such as certified public accountants, stock brokers, or even bankers, also utilize the units of the condominium complex in the same manner.

Street-level shops of such condominiums may be sold to retail outlets such as pharmacies, laboratory service groups, or restaurants and general retail shops.

The *industrial park* is a special kind of commercial condominium in which a number of different buildings housing companies are constructed together in a specially landscaped area. Each separate company owns its building or buildings and in addition owns an undivided interest in the common property of the industrial park, such as parking lots, grounds, sidewalks, shopping areas, and shares maintenance and management fees of these areas through membership in the overall owners' association.

Construction of the industrial park is a widespread phenomenon in many growing suburban communities. Its success has been stimulated by the precipitate flight of huge business concerns from urban areas burdened with heavy taxation and transportation problems.

Who Wants a Commercial Condominium? The condominium concept has introduced a whole new way of doing business to professionals and company owners. At one time the doctor or lawyer was unable to purchase an office, but was forced to rent, leaving himself at the mercy of his landlord.

Most businessmen find that owning condo office space costs less than renting office space. The reason for this is that the increased federal tax shelter affords him the use of a depreciation deduction. All income-producing properties owned—for example, the office space itself—can be depreciated over a reasonable time span for an IRS deduction, which means a lower tax. When renting, the landlord benefits from this depreciation, not the renter

And the condo owner enjoys the added benefit of growth of his equity, appreciation of his resale value, and assurance that any change in design and installation will add to the value of his office space.

The office condo owner can also join together with other owners in the office condominium association to determine what if any use restrictions ought to be placed on the building. As a member of the association, he has the right to control the way in which the building is managed avoiding such problems as unsatisfactory maintenance.

... 4

Comparison Shopping

SHOPPING for the right condominium is certainly a more important consideration than shopping for a car, but at the same time it is also a matter of comparing one feature against another, and then deciding on whether or not the difference in cost is commensurate with the quality or the model and make you want.

There are two criteria important in any of the comparisons you will make between condominium life and rental life, between condominium life and cooperative apartment life, between condominium life and single-family house life. They are financial and personal.

Although your personal reactions are of primary consideration to you and will be accorded a great deal of weight in your own mind when you come to your final decision, financial considerations are of paramount importance. They will affect your considerations in the final analysis.

We'll be comparison shopping between condominium life and three other lifestyles: rented apartment, owned cooperative apartment, owned single-family house.

RENTED APARTMENT

You may be one of the many people who have always lived in rented apartments and who seem to thrive on the experience. Single or married—even with children—you may find the lifestyle completely enjoyable.

For example, you may like the freedom from chores and household duties that would occupy you if you owned your own home. And you may like your independence as a renter; that is, if you become disenchanted with the management of a certain apartment, you can always look for another and move out. You may also like the ambiance that belongs to life in the city, close to the center of culture, near to thousands of other people, next to the heart-throb of urban life.

Yet you have thought about buying a condominium unit in the suburbs. You've heard a lot about the tax breaks you get when you own property. But you'd like to know exactly what it will cost and what you're going to be getting for your money.

So . . .

Assume for the moment that you are paying $400 a month for rent. Also assume that you are making a salary that puts you in the 30 percent tax bracket. Because you are a renter, you cannot deduct real estate taxes or mortgage interest that would be your privilege if you owned your own living unit in a condominium.

If you purchase a condominium unit for a like amount of outgo—that is, if your mortgage and real estate taxes were equal to $4,800 a year—you will be benefitted by several considerations.

CONDOMINIUM BENEFITS

Mortgage Interest Deduction. You will first of all be able to deduct the amount of interest you pay on your mortgage throughout the year. In the early months of mortgage payments, most of the amount paid is interest. You might be able to deduct $3,300 of the $3,600 mortgage payments in computing your income tax the first year.

Since you are in the 30 percent tax bracket, you will avoid paying $990 in taxes! To put it another way, your total mortgage payments come to only $2,610.

Real Estate Tax Deduction. In addition, you will also be able to deduct your real estate tax payments for the year from your gross income. With your real estate tax coming to $1,200 a year, and your deduction in the 30 percent bracket, you will save an actual $360.

Combining your actual saving on your mortgage interest deduction—$990—and on your real estate tax assessment—$360—you will save a total of $1,350.

Instead of paying out $4,800 as you would in renting an apartment, you will be paying out only $3,440 per year—and investing your money in your condominium property to boot!

Your Equity Buildup. The biggest advantage in owning your own condo unit is that the money put into the mortgage actually *buys* you something that you own yourself. Of the $3,600 you pay the first year, $300 goes to pay off the principal of the mortgage, as we have seen. That $300 becomes applied to your ownership of the property. It is your "equity," the amount of the living unit you actually own at the end of the first year of payment.

Later on, the proportion of each mortgage payment shifts from predominantly interest to predominantly principal. Your principal payoff increases month to month—so, too, does your equity. By the time you pay off your mortgage, you have complete equity in the condo property.

If you decide to sell your property at any time, the equity is yours. In other words, if you buy a condominium unit for $50,000, using a $10,000 down payment and taking out a $40,000 mortgage, within five years you have earned perhaps $8,000 in equity. You still owe $32,000 on the mortgage, but own equity amounting to $18,000 ($10,000 + $8,000).

If you sell the condominium unit for $65,000—most condo properties escalate with inflation—you would then make a profit of $23,000. The *apparent* profit of $33,000 ($65,000 − $32,000) must be reduced by $10,000, the original down payment you made when you bought the property. Your *actual* profit is $23,000, as stated.

$100,000 Tax-Free Home Sale. Maybe you've held off buying a condominium unit or a single-family house because you've heard how much the capital gains tax takes off any profit you might make from selling the condo. Actually, the only time you might make a profit when you sell a condo is one time in your life: when you have just sent your last offspring out into the world and the two of you are rattling around in a half-empty unit. You sell the condo for a smaller, cheaper one.

The difference between the sale of the condo and the cost of the purchase of a smaller unit is a profit, and must be considered a capital gain. Any other time you sell one condo and move into another, you are probably moving from a smaller to a larger—hence from a cheaper to a more expensive—home and will not make a profit at all.

Yet now, even the capital gain you make on that one-time sale of the bigger condo or house to purchase the smaller condo is *not* going to cost you tax money. The 1978 Revenue Act affords you a fantastic tax break in the form of a once-in-a-lifetime chance to exclude from your income up to $100,000 of any profit on the sale of your principal residence. "Principal residence" includes condominiums, cooperative apartments, and single-family homes.

There are several stipulations necessary for you to take advantage of this tax break:

• You must be at least fifty-five years old when you make the sale of the house, condominium, or cooperative apartment.

• The condominium unit must be your principal residence. If you own a time-shared condominium which you occupy for only a month or two during the year, that is not your principal residence. You cannot, therefore, exclude from the tax any profit you make on the sale of the time-shared condominium.

• If you were fifty-five or over but not yet sixty-five when you make the sale, you must have owned and used the condo property as your principal residence for a period totaling three years or more during the five-year span ending on the date you sell or exchange it.

• If you are sixty-five or over when you make the sale—and the sale is completed before July 26, 1981—you can qualify if you owned and occupied the property as your principal residence for five out of eight years before the sale, even if you don't meet the three-out-of-five-year test.

Note that this is strictly a one-shot, once-in-a-lifetime break, much in the same manner that the Veterans Administration-insured loan is a once-in-a-lifetime break for a qualified war veteran. Once you decide on the sale or exchange of your principal residence, you cannot make a similar deal for any subsequent sale or exchange of a future principal residence.

Suppose you purchase a principal condo residence for $25,000 and sell it for $50,000 to move into a smaller apartment. If you qualify, you can elect to exclude your $25,000 profit from tax. If you do, that's your one-shot exclusion. You can't make any later choice to protect another $75,000 of profit from tax—even though you didn't use up the full amount of your $100,000 exclusion right

In other words, if you give up your condo after severa
years and buy another for $50,000, then sell that cond
after living in it for the required time at $100,000, yo
would make $50,000 on the sale. However, you canno
exclude this $50,000 profit from tax because you prev
ously used up your once-in-a-lifetime election on the $25
000 profit from the sale of your last condo.

The point is to think long and hard before decidin
when to use your one-shot election.

If you expect to sell your condo in the future, keep th
new tax-free option clearly in mind. You may, for exam
ple, be a fifty-four-year-old condo owner. You can an
want to sell your suburban condo at $100,000 profit, wit
the intention of moving into a smaller condo in the city
If you do this before you become fifty-five, your entir
$100,000 profit will be taxable as a capital gain. If you hol
off selling until you reach the age of fifty-five, you may no
be able to make $100,000 on the condo because of
deterioration of the housing market or a serious change i
home-selling conditions in your area that results in
lower profit for you.

These possibilities must always be considered. Th
point is that with the entire profit taxable, your choice
unmistakable. Hold off until you reach fifty-five.

WHAT TO DO ABOUT CONVERSION?

The ability to compare both financial and personal ac
vantages and disadvantages between renting an apar
ment and owning a condominium unit becomes of pr
mary importance if you, as a renter, are suddenly face
with a conversion notice.

Conversion of rental apartments to condominium uni

has been widespread throughout the country for the past several years. Such conversions occur every day. Far fewer rental apartments are being built now than in the mid-1970s.

As costs keep rising for landlords who own rental apartments, more and more of them opt to convert to condominium units and sell out. It is estimated that the owner of a rental apartment building usually makes a profit of at least 20 percent by converting his rental units to condo units.

Let's suppose you are a renter, and your building goes condo.

Buying your own rental apartment can be a costly, scary operation. And buying is largely an upper-income phenomenon. Mortgage and maintenance costs sometimes come to as much as 50 percent more than renting the same space. However, there are advantages.

In certain areas, condominium units have been appreciating in value at an annual rate of 14 or 15 percent. At the same time, single-family homes have been going up at only 12 percent. In Chicago one three-bedroom unit valued at $55,000 in 1974 was worth $110,000 in early 1979. That's a 100 percent rise—20 percent a year.

If you are faced with conversion, you have to think about it, of course, and compare the advantages with the disadvantages. But if you are like most people in the same spot, and if you have the money, you'll buy your first condo apartment.

Nevertheless, you must prepare to pay substantially more each month as a condo owner than as a renter—and it's all money up front. For example, in January 1979 a Chicago rental apartment at $280 a month was converted to a condominium unit selling for $58,000—roughly seventeen times the yearly amount of rent! Another, renting at $360 several years ago, was sold for $85,000—roughly nineteen times the yearly rent! A Santa Monica apartment renting at $395 a month sold for $95,000—nearly twenty times the yearly amount of rent! On the other hand, an apartment at $270 a month in Chicago was converted into a condo at $50,000—only a little over eleven times the yearly rent.

That $58,000 one-bedroom condo was sold with a 10 percent down payment. The costs of amortization, including monthly assessment and real estate taxes, ran $606.25. The owner, who was in a 30 percent tax bracket, wound up paying $443 (with income tax deductions for interest and real estate figured in) compared with the $280 he paid for the same unit as a rental.

But even though each condo owner paid more per month, he was building equity in property that was rapidly escalating in value—making him a good, solid profit.

CONDOMINIUMS AND COOPERATIVES

The difference between buying a cooperative apartment and a condominium unit isn't really very great. Cooperatives traditionally have been much more popular in New York City than condominiums. Many of them are located in and around Manhattan, but they can also be found in other large urban areas throughout the country.

If you like the apartment and want to buy it, there is little reason you shouldn't—whether it be a cooperative apartment or a condominium unit. Basically, there are only one or two differences between co-ops and condos.

They both enjoy the same attractive tax advantages— the same as those afforded homeowners—your being able to deduct interest and property taxes.

As a condominium owner you actually *own* the interior of your living unit, plus a proportionate share in all com-

mon property of the condominium project. As a cooperative owner, you do *not* own your unit outright, but a share
in the corporation that owns the entire property; this in
turn is owned and run jointly by its shareholders.

With a co-op, you hold a "proprietary lease"—like a
regular apartment rental lease—on the specific apartment you occupy within the complex and pay your proportionate share in the cooperative's expenses.

In practice, however, the two modes of ownership are
in many ways identical. Two important differences are:

• As a condominium owner, you pay a monthly fee to
the condominium management for maintenance of the
common property while you pay the monthly mortgage
payment on your unit to the bank. As a cooperative
owner, you pay both your monthly fee for the maintenance of the cooperative and the amount of your share of
the co-op mortgage to the management.

• As a condominium owner, you're generally *not* responsible for a neighbor's default—except that you help
pay the extra accumulated maintenance costs that may
result. In a cooperative, you share the financial responsibility for individual defaults with other members.

Condos in many areas tend to appreciate faster in the
real estate market today because most buyers can get
mortgage financing at cheaper rates than co-op buyers.

There is a reason for this. The cooperative apartment
buyer must take out a *personal* loan at higher interest
than a mortgage loan since he owns *shares* of property
that are not mortgageable individually. The cooperative
apartment owner, remember, does not take out a mortgage loan at all; he pays his share of a larger one covering
the entire building.

In addition, cooperatives are more restrictive than condominiums—at least most experts in the field say so. Individual co-op and condo owners may disagree. By and

large, however, the cooperative is run on bylaws that are more tightly controlled than the bylaws of the typical condominium.

The co-op's board of directors must approve a potential buyer before he can acquire shares in the corporation. A condominium unit can be sold to whomever the owner chooses, provided there is no "first refusal" clause in the bylaws.

However, the differences between co-ops and condos are infinitesimal in comparison to the differences between rental apartments and co-ops and condos.

SINGLE-FAMILY HOME

The condo unit owner and the single-family house owner have much in common from a legal and financial standpoint, but they have an entirely different kind of lifestyle—even if they happen to live next door to each other.

There are financial advantages to condominium ownership. The condo unit is generally cheaper than a single-family house, because many of the costs are shared by all unit owners. The cost of maintenance and upkeep on a one-acre high-rise condominium will be shared by possibly fifty individual owners, whereas the cost of maintenance and upkeep on a one-acre single-family house is a one-person responsibility! The comparison, while a bit far-fetched, does give you an example of what to think about when weighing the two types of ownership.

Here is a more solid, more practical comparison. The cost of the average condominium unit in December 1978 was $42,850. The cost of the average single-family home at the same time was $61,000. That's 42 percent more expensive—almost one-half more!

Similarities between condo purchase and single-family house purchase are many. Both sales transactions involve signing an initial sales contract. Both involve procuring a mortgage loan, unless, of course, you pay cash—which few do! Both involve arranging for a down payment, which is usually less for a condominium than for a home. Both involve signing a complex set of legal papers at a closing.

However, there are implied obligations which you undertake when you purchase a condominium that are not involved in the purchase of a house. It is very important that you understand these before you find yourself inadvertently shirking them.

THE OBLIGATIONS OF THE CONDO UNIT OWNER

The most important of these is your obligation to share control, along with your fellow unit owners, of the operation of the condominium through the board of directors of the homeowners association. This operation includes the budgeting of all maintenance and upkeep costs and all fixed costs such as insurance and liability. Although many condo owners avoid "getting involved" in the association government, they do so at their own risk. Condominium life is based on the same kind of cooperative endeavor that small-town life in early Colonial days was based on. Avoid becoming involved with the day-to-day running of the condominium at your peril!

The second most important of these obligations is a financial one. It is your agreement to pay your proportionate share of maintaining and operating all jointly owned property, such as elevators, garages, and swimming pools. If mismanagement occurs, you share in the loss. There is no way in which you can legally avoid paying these monthly maintenance fees. If you do fail to pay them, there is a clause in the bylaws that allows the board of directors to place a lien on your property.

The third obligation is your agreement to pay all special assessments voted upon by a majority of owners. Emergencies do come up, even in the best-run condominiums. Such assessments might be needed for the following contingencies:

• Repairs to the building and grounds following a fire, flood, hurricane, or earthquake, when available insurance and other funds cannot meet full restoration costs.

• Renovation and improvement expenses, particularly to an older project that has come to the point where normal repairs are inadequate.

• Purchase of individual units by the homeowners association when a foreclosure occurs and an outside buyer is not immediately available.

• Annual assessments uncollected because of the default of one or more of the condominium owners.

Most of the general differences between owning a single-family house and a condominium unit have been discussed in detail in Chapters 1 and 3.

...5

Checklist for Buyers

LIKE any piece of real estate property, the condominium must be thoroughly investigated and analyzed before making a decision to buy. But because of certain aspects peculiar to the condominium—the use of common facilities, for example—a typical checklist for the buyer is of necessity somewhat longer than a checklist for the purchase of a home.

Let's begin the checklist with the primary appeal of the condominium—its visual image.

HOW DOES THE CONDOMINIUM LOOK?

The visual appeal of the condominium structure is of exceptional importance to you when you are thinking of buying a place. It will set the tone for anyone visiting you later on; guests will see it first and you second.

It is not only essential that the building itself be of good and tasteful design, but the setting must be compatible with the structure. Proper blending of the two can make all the difference between a good unit and a bad one.

Note first how the architect has designed the structure. Has he produced a building that has a satisfying appearance, with all elements harmonious with the environment? Has he given the overall project a sense of variety?

Does the condominium have a natural appeal to it, or does the sight of it jangle the nerves?

Be sure all common entrances are spacious and comfortable. Has the architect protected the privacy of each unit owner by the use of exclusive entrances or courtyards? Does the general appearance of the structure have the proper ambiance you are after? If not—think twice. There is nothing worse than living in a place you don't like the sight of.

Now note how the landscape designer has arranged the setting around the structure. Has he thrown in a couple of shrubs and trees for an instant landscape job? Or has he made an imaginative and conscientious effort to create a pleasing image with plants along the walkways, curved paths, benches, varied ground levels, interesting lighting effects, large and small trees placed for balance, and hedges in imaginative plantings?

Has he put the parking areas out of the way so that they do not interfere with the view of the condominium from the front? Has he prepared the grounds around the condominium proper so that it blends in with the neighboring projects?

Now close your eyes and try to think of the entire site as it will be when it is filled with people. Visualize the swimming pool with several people there. Think of the noise. Imagine the parking lot full of cars. It will be crowded eventually, even if it is not now. Try to think ahead and determine if it's what you want.

Now compare the project with the neighboring structures around it. Is it better? Is it the same? Is it less attractive? Is it noncompetitive? Actually, the project should be *better* than its neighbors but not *too* much better. At any rate, it should *fit in* and not be obtrusive.

WHERE IS THE CONDOMINIUM LOCATED?

As important as the overall visual image of the condominium to the outside world is its location and the status of the neighborhood directly contiguous to it.

How close is the condominium to a good shopping area? Are there any cultural attractions nearby? Where are the schools in relation to its location? Are there other recreation facilities available in addition to those furnished by the condominium itself?

You must balance the effect of the condo's location with other factors. For example, if the location of the condominium is ideal for your purposes, you can overlook a lot of other features which might not be first-rate. However, if the location is not very good, and has a number of undesirable features, even the best of additional facilities in the project itself cannot make the purchase of a unit in the building in any way desirable.

In analyzing the location, pay considerable attention to the status of the surrounding community—that is, the neighborhood in which the condominium is located. Rarely do neighborhoods stay constant. They either improve or degenerate. If the neighborhood is in the process of improving, you should have little trouble in selling the condominium at a higher price in the near future. However, if the neighborhood is going down, the amount of money for which you can sell the unit may be even less than what you are required to pay originally.

Learn as much as you can about the buildings, houses, and shopping centers near the condominium. If the single-family homes nearby have been selling for consistently rising prices, the neighborhood is improving. If the prices for rental apartments have been rising, the same is true. If the shopping center has been expanding, it is obvious that the neighborhood is doing well.

If, on the other hand, there are a number of homes with "For Sale" signs out front, if there are apartment units going unrented in many of the nearby buildings, and if the shopping areas are full of empty store space, the neighborhood is in a state of deterioration.

One good place to check out the viability of a neighborhood is in the school system. Are the buildings old or new? Are they kept up or are they going to pieces?

Urban and suburban rot spreads out from the center of any community. You can even anticipate a neighborhood which may deteriorate in the future by a careful study of a city map.

Note the areas of deterioration. You will find that they usually start at or near the center of the community. Such an area will radiate out from the center, moving slowly in an almost direct line like the spokes of a wheel. If the property you are considering lies in the path of one of the spreading tentacles of deterioration, the chances are that eventually that property will begin to fail and join in the creeping urban or suburban decay. Obviously, the closer the property lies to the deteriorated section, the faster it can face degeneration.

If the property you are considering lies in the opposite direction of such blight, the chances are good that it will not be afflicted in the near future. In that case, you should be able to live well in the condominium and sell out before property values begin to drop.

How Are the Condo Units Selling?

Another way to determine the true value of a condominium property is to investigate the number of sales of units and the speed of these sales. A successful condominium project always has a high degree of sales—sometimes causing a quick sellout of all units in several days.

Quick turnover can mean a very great deal to you. It means that if you have to move somewhere else and want to sell your unit, you will be able to find a buyer quickly and easily. It also means that you probably will be able to get more for your property than you paid for it. Sales activity can also mean that the neighborhood itself is a good one and will remain prosperous in the future.

If there is little positive response to a heavy sales campaign for the condominium project, you could be in for trouble. If no one is interested in living in it, there must be something wrong with its appeal. It might be overpriced, unaesthetic generally, or in a poor location.

However, you must analyze these factors honestly. What does not appeal to someone else may very well appeal to you. Yet there is a drawback in that case. If the condo unit attracts you enough to make you want to buy it, but doesn't appeal to anyone else, how are you going to be able to sell it in the future if you should want to move somewhere else?

A low activity of sales is a warning of another danger. If the best units in the condominium are all purchased and sales slack off, there is a real danger that the remaining units may not be sold. A condominium with units unsold is not a desirable place to live: with fewer owners, each will have to pay higher rates for maintenance. Besides, the builder may panic and rent out the unsold units, reducing the sales potential of your living unit.

A good rule of thumb in analyzing condominium sales activity is to assume that if the condo offering has been on the market for more than nine months and has sold only half of the units available the project is not going to sell out in the near future.

It is wise to check carefully to find out if any of the rates of the unsold units have been lowered in order to stimulate sales. Stable or slightly rising prices indicate a successful venture. Falling prices indicate the opposite.

When you check the location of the already sold units you may see that they are all on the side of the structure with the best view. Why aren't any of the units with less attractive locations sold? There should be a balance of both. If only the best are sold, it could mean that the project as a whole isn't too good.

Also, if all the units sold are the same type—all lower-priced units or all two-bedroom units—that means that there is going to be a problem selling the remaining units of the project. The ideal situation is one in which the unit sales are evenly distributed throughout the building. That means that the whole project has excellent potential and may well be a sellout.

ARE THE ZONING LAWS FAVORABLE?

Another important point to check out before making your decision to buy is the status of the zoning laws regarding adjacent property. You can usually find zoning maps at the city hall. When checking on the zoning situation around the condominium you are interested in, you should make sure there are no areas zoned for business or other types of construction. Actually, the zoning around the property should be multiunit residential housing exclusively. If, however, the zoning nearby is restricted to single-family houses, you are in luck.

You should also check to make sure that no new building projects are planned for the area. High-rises and other crowded structures could easily limit your privacy, your view, and drive down your resale prospects.

Although zoning maps don't usually show it, you should check out the traffic on roads and highways nearby, bus and train routes, overhead air traffic, and commuter and automobile traffic.

How Much Does It Cost?

Although there are no hard and fast rules these days on real estate costs, since prices fluctuate so rapidly during periods of inflation, most condominium units are priced competitively with other offerings, such as single-family homes, apartment rental units, and cooperatives.

A condo price can run 10 to 30 percent less than the price of a comparable single-family home in the same neighborhood. In comparing prices, you also must consider the common facilities available to condo owners: swimming pool, tennis courts, and so on.

If you compare condominium monthly costs before federal tax deductions with rental rates for similar units, condo costs run anywhere from 25 percent to 50 percent higher, but total income tax savings can shave that difference considerably.

In a high-rise condo prices vary from floor to floor and from view to view. The higher you go, oddly enough, the more the unit costs. A price increase of 1 to 3 percent from floor to floor is not unusual. At the same time, prices may vary up to 20 percent on the same floor because of view, location, or noise considerations. However, in walk-ups prices for third-floor units can be up to 5 to 15 percent lower than first and second levels.

It is a good idea in the case of a resale to find out when the original unit was sold and what its price was. By comparing the figures with an appropriate sales-value appreciation rate per year for the neighborhood, you can determine the appropriate maximum resale price.

If the offering price far exceeds the figure you determine, don't buy unless the higher value can be justified. Improvements, additions, and other factors such as location and neighborhood may make the figure justifiable. On the other hand, if the offering price isn't much more than the original sales price, that can mean that the neighborhood, the building, or the entire area may be in trouble. Do you want to buy into a depreciating situation?

To Whom Can You Sell It?

If you buy, you must always think about selling. If you wanted to sell the unit, to whom would you sell it? Is there a potential buyer for the unit available?

If you are a young married couple or a single person, you would feel odd moving into a building filled with retirees. And if you were a retiree, you would not like to move into a building full of small children and newly marrieds.

There are also restrictions in certain projects that would lock out families with children, older people, people with pets, and so on. Be sure you understand what restrictions there are in the unit you want to buy.

How Is the Condo Laid Out?

The way in which the architect lays out the condominium facilities is very important in determining the quality of a project. Since most of the facilities are to be in common use by everyone in the project, it is of primary concern exactly where they are located.

A good way to qualify these common facilities is to use the checklist provided.

1. If the project has a front entranceway, determine whether or not it has a quality two-way intercom system for security purposes. Many condos provide not only electronic surveillance, but have full-time, twenty-four-hour doorman service as well.

2. Be sure that all public and private entrances into the project are adequately secured with double-lock systems, and, if possible, electronic surveillance as well.

3. The best projects have service entrances placed in the rear of the building. It is a great inconvenience to owners of units to have service calls made in the front of the building.

4. The lobby of the project should be airy, illuminated, spacious, and comfortable. It should be designed so that it is compatible with the overall decor of the building.

5. Laundry rooms, game rooms, elevators, stairwells, and other common facilities should be located in sites where they do not interfere with nearby units.

6. The elevator itself in a high-rise project is extremely important. It should ride smoothly, swiftly, and must make even stops with all floors, including lower parking levels.

7. Laundry facilities must be offered in an easily accessible, centrally located site. Community rooms, saunas, locker rooms, and individual storage spaces in the basement may also be provided.

8. Be sure there are removal facilities for garbage and trash. These must be accessible for the convenience of the owners. And there should be an adequate property drainage system that will prevent flooding.

In checking out each of the preceding, be sure to investigate them for practical usage. For example, the project may have a central laundry facility—but it may include only three machines for seventy-five unit owners! Or, the project may provide storage space, but after you check it over you may find that there is only a 4-by-5-foot space available!

You should also investigate all the larger recreational amenities, such as swimming pools and tennis courts. These facilities are the major attractions of the condominium. The size and depth of the pool and the number and type of tennis courts may be not at all what you have been led to believe.

In the case of a new condo, the recreational facilities may not even be constructed yet. It is important to determine the time schedule for the construction of these facilities. In the builder's mind these have the lowest construction priority of all; in the buyer's they may easily be the highest.

How Are the Condo's Furnishings?

A condominium unit should offer the same furnishings and appliances that an ordinary house does, in addition to all the commonly shared facilities. But many people forget about them in their excitement over seeing the Olympic-sized swimming pool and the giant billiard room.

Be sure to investigate and analyze the condominium's offerings from the standpoint of the ordinary household amenities you would expect.

• Are the rooms spacious? Is there enough natural light and ventilation? Is air-conditioning available? Are the heating units well placed? Are the walls insulated? Are the windows weather-stripped?

• Are there floor plan options available? How are the bathroom and kitchen areas for accessibility and usage? Is the bathroom an eyesore, visible from the living room?

Are the bedrooms properly arranged for quietness and seclusion?

• Has the unit been designed with versatility of room use in mind? Can a bedroom substitute for a study or den? Can a guest room become a nursery?

• Has the unit been designed with the proper thought to privacy? Can you get away from everyone else if you want to? Is there plenty of protection from common halls and walkways?

• Examine the kitchen appliances and bathroom facilities carefully. Are they the kind you would want to own in a single-family home? Are the appliances and facilities included in the sale? If not, are there adequate fittings for hookups? Are they located in the right places?

• Are the electricity, heat, and gas metered individually in every condominium unit? If it is not, how is the sharing of such utilities determined? Can you be sure you won't be charged for someone else's overuse of power or heat?

• Are there exhaust fans in the kitchen to blow out cooking smoke and odors? Are there vents to take care of excessive heat in summertime? Does the chimney really work?

• If carpeting is available on the floor, check it thoroughly. Is it adequately padded? Will you have to provide your own padding? Are the floor areas adequately carpeted?

• Noise is a bothersome factor in any multiple-dwelling building. Are the walls soundproofed so that noise from adjoining units won't come through? Check to see that ample noise dampening has been provided in the ceilings and floors to keep noise from units above and below.

"I CAN'T PARK THE CAR IN THE FAMILY ROOM"

One of the most important considerations for most condominium owners is the availability of a large, adequate parking area.

Make sure that the condo *does* offer a common parking facility. Make sure also that the condominium itself—that is, you with the other unit owners—owns the parking area. Check the space. Be sure that every unit owner has his own private space and that he will be able to park his car somewhere at any time.

Also be sure that the parking lot is within a short walking distance of your own unit. At the same time, it shouldn't be out in the open in such a way that it ruins the aesthetic lines of the condominium's profile.

In many new projects, the parking facilities are located downstairs in the basement. Make sure that the driveways are adequately sloped and curved to prevent fender-bender accidents when you are coming in or driving out.

...6

Condo Traps—Beware!

THERE are pitfalls and traps into which the unwary can blunder in almost any kind of real estate transaction. Because of the novelty and unfamiliarity of the condominium, condo buying is fraught with hidden gimmicks that are unknown to many otherwise sophisticated people.

Some of these "traps" have already been touched upon. Others have not. In the following chapter these pitfalls have been arranged one after the other so you can see at a glance the most important and serious of them.

For every trap or pitfall there is a defense provided to safeguard you against being burned—either financially or psychologically. Both explanation and defense are discussed briefly. Further information may be obtained, in some instances, in other portions of the book.

Trap #1: The Recreational Lease. A builder may retain ownership to parts of a condominium project, in particular the recreational facilities, and sometimes even the land, to lease them back to the buyers for ninety-nine years. The problem is that you may find the lease rates rise in response to inflation and other factors, subjecting you to exorbitant charges over an extended period of time. In some cases, failure to pay such an obligation may result in loss of your unit through foreclosure. Although legal in a state that does not have a law against leaseholds, such a lease-back gimmick can add up to a large outlay of money over the years and should be avoided if possible.

Defense Against Rec-Lease Abuse. The obvious solution to the problem is to refuse to buy into any condominium with a leasehold clause in its papers. However, it is not quite that simple. In some instances the leasehold arrangement may be provided to make payment of the condominium unit lower. Some salespeople offer that argument even if it isn't true. You have to make up your own mind about whether or not to buy. The "trap" is nevertheless one you should investigate thoroughly should you discover it in your contract.

Trap #2: Underestimated Expenses. In the early months of a condominium's existence, when it is still being managed by the builder/developer, there is a tendency for the builder to make the maintenance and upkeep expenses look fantastically low—to "lowball" the monthly cost, in real estate parlance. Since the builder has full control of the operating budget, he simply pays for some going expenses out of his own pocket—to make the maintenance fees look small. As soon as control of the condo is handed over to the owners, the fees escalate dramatically, causing untold misery in otherwise cautious buyers.

Defense Against Lowballing Fees. Examine the operating budget carefully, trying to determine whether or not the cost of mainenance compares with the types of upkeep costs you see as you look over the development: clubhouse maintenance; grounds maintenance; swimming pool; security; building itself; parking area. There will be some escalation of fees, following the normal inflation curve, but you don't want to be too surprised once you move in and assume responsibility as a unit owner.

Trap #3: Right of First Refusal. Many condominium associations do not allow you to sell your condominium on the open market. You must first offer it to the association for approval of the prospective buyer. "Right of first refusal" is the way this clause is sometimes worded. Actually it is an out-and-out restriction of your resale rights. No matter how this restriction is stated, it clearly contradicts "fee simple ownership," which carries with it the undisputed right of disposal.

Defense Against Selling Restrictions. No FHA-regulated condominium allows any language at all that restricts the resale rights of owners. "Right of first refusal" is not prohibited in some state statutes, but it is specifically prohibited in condominiums having FHA-insured mortgages. If you do find restrictions in your contract, be sure you know exactly what they entail. You may not be permitted to sell to anyone with children under 16 or pets. Know the contract before you sign.

Trap #4: Expensive Projected Amenities. The builder/developer may intend to enlarge the condominium by building more buildings or adding rental units. He may also intend to add additional recreational facilities that could raise maintenance and upkeep fees. All these additional projections could cost you money—possibly staggering amounts.

Defense Against Future Fees and Assessments. Be on guard when you see that a specific percentage of interest in your condominium unit has not yet been specified on the contract. Find out exactly what the builder's intentions are. The addition of commercial units will not raise the value of your unit—nor will added rental units. Ask where the boundaries of the condominium's common estate are located, and if there are any restricted common areas—such as undeveloped land—and how they apply to you. Determine the extent of any other control the builder has, both before and after the condominium is legally constituted, and what effect, if any, it has on your future rights and obligations.

Trap #5: Transient Occupancy. A builder may retain the right to rent or lease units he still owns for what is called "transient purposes"—that is, short periods of time such as one night to a week (anything less than thirty days). Or, he may provide services generally considered "customary hotel services." Transient occupancy can cause security problems, damage to recreational facilities, and a general depreciation of the entire condominium.

Defense Against Hotel Service. Developments with federally insured mortgages do not allow rentals for transient or hotel purposes. However, you should have the right to lease or rent out your own unit for residential purposes, subject to whatever restrictions are contained in the declaration or bylaws. Avoid buying into a condominium project that retains the right to transient occupancy.

Trap #6: Casualty Gap. The fire, theft, and other casualty coverage may be entirely adequate in the master insurance plan as far as it relates to the common areas of the condominium. However, coverage may not include any of the "space estate" inside your own living unit. Thus, if your unit is destroyed in a fire that takes the building, the common property is covered but your own things are not!

Defense Against Casualty Shortages. Look for such gaps in the master insurance plan, and make sure that you are covered separately in your own unit.

Trap #7: Liability Gap. Likewise, liability coverage may be adequate in the master insurance plan as far as it relates to the common areas in the condominium. But it probably does not include your own condo unit. If someone falls in your unit, or has reason to sue you for liability within your unit, you should realize you are not covered by the "common property" plan.

Defense Against Liability Shortages. Look for such gaps in the master insurance plan, and make sure that you are covered separately in your own unit.

Trap #8: Insufficient Condo Coverage. A condominium with insufficient casualty, hazard, and liability insurance coverage can be subject to staggering losses due to fire, flood, accident, and other perils. As a co-owner in the common property of the condominium, you are subject to liability charges as well.

Defense Against Insufficient Insurance. Make sure that the policy contains a condominium property endorsement that recognizes that condominiums have a multiple number of beneficiaries. Make certain that such an endorsement is part of the insurance package. Also make sure that the liability insurance policy names, as insured, the board of directors and each unit owner individually as a co-owner.

Trap #9: Disappearing Down Payment Ploy. In a projected condominium the developer may plan to use your down payment to purchase material or pay labor costs on the construction of the condominium. In the event the project falls through by failure of the builder to sell all the units, you will lose your initial down payment.

Defense Against Down Payment Abuse. Make the builder deposit your down payment in escrow until the condominium and grounds are substantially completed. Federal Housing Administration loans and some state laws require the builder to deposit all down payment money in escrow. Others do not. Be sure also that you know exactly how the builder plans to finance the construction of the condominium common facilities before you give him any money. Don't forget that the price of your living unit includes not only the part where you live, but also a proportionate amount of the common area and its facilities.

Trap #10: The "Incredible Shrinking Unit" Ploy. When you sign up for a projected living unit in a contemplated condominium that is still in the planning stage, it is possible that the finished living unit you are paying for does not resemble what you thought you were getting. In fact, it may be only a small microcosm of what has been promised you.

Defense Against Substitute Unit. When you sign the sales contract, make sure that you have *in writing* exactly what you're getting: the size and specific features of your unit, the construction quality, and the expected completion date. If there is a model unit available for inspection, look at it carefully so you will get no nasty surprises when you finally move in.

Trap #11: The "Pie in the Sky" Dodge. Promised recreational facilities may not yet be built when you sign up for your condominium unit. Such facilities are an important part of your condominium lifestyle, but are simply "pie in the sky" at the time you sign up for them.

Defense Against Promises, Promises. There are three points to cover:

• Be sure the builder has the necessary permits to get them built. Also, make sure he has sufficient land and that it is suitable for what he plans.

• Find out whether he has the right to cancel any of these planned facilities if he doesn't sell enough units.

• Ask the builder whether he can charge you additional assessments—over and above the monthly assessment estimate—in order to cover your obligation to them.

Trap #12: The High-Pressure Sales Contract. Yielding to high-pressure tactics and signing a sales contract before you fully understand what you are buying may cost you dearly. Later on you may find out that there are hidden costs or obligations you did not know about because you did not take time to ask.

Defense Against Sales Pressure. Carefully review the sales contract before you sign. Look especially for anything that binds you unreasonably or ratifies organizational documents you have not read, such as the enabling declaration, bylaws, and so on. Ask about any liability that you must assume for extras, whatever they are. Don't take a chance on losing all your money through careless disregard of small print!

Trap #13: The "Wham-Bam" Sales Ploy. Not only the sales contract, but all the basic condominium documents —enabling declaration, bylaws, purchase agreement— should be studied carefully before you agree to buy. Beware the salesperson who wants you to read, reread, digest, and understand these documents in five or ten minutes.

Defense Against Quickie Signing. Salespeople love to close deals quickly. Look out for the one who wants you to sign a purchase agreement without even reading it. Be doubly suspicious of any salesperson who advises you to sign without reading the more complicated documents of the condominium project—enabling declaration, bylaws, purchase agreement.

Make him give you a "decent waiting period"—it can be up to ten days if you want that much—to read, reread, digest, and understand these documents. In fact, it is a good idea to turn all these papers over to a lawyer for him to study as well. Never allow any salesperson, even if he is a friend of yours, to hustle you into a hasty, thoughtless act that may be the most important decision you make in your life.

Trap #14: Long-Term Agreements. The builder may try to lock you into long-term agreements or self-serving covenants in order to establish the condominium legally and financially.

Defense Against Long-Term Restrictions. Object to any covenant that restricts your rights to make your own decisions through your board of directors. This is especially true of any agreement that will affect the marketability of your living unit.

Trap #15: The Management Company Ploy. The builder may seek to retain extended control over the condominium project by establishing a management company entirely independent of the condominium project and then hiring the management company during the first months of the condominium's operation, when he is still in control. With a long-term, noncancelable contract effectively signed, he can retain control indefinitely.

Defense Against Permanent Control Gimmicks. Study the documents carefully. Be sure that there is no clause in the declaration that allows the builder to retain control of the condominium through direct power in a management company he controls.

Trap #16: The "Ghost Manager" Ploy. A switch on Number 15 is the "ghost manager" ploy. Here the builder retains extended control over the project by hiring a manager during the first months of the condominium's management and signing him to a long-term, noncancelable contract. At the same time, the builder becomes a silent "ghost" partner of the manager!

Defense Against "Ghost Manager." Make sure that there is a clause in the documents that allows the board of directors of the association the exclusive right to hire and/or fire the condominium manager at any time. Stipulation should *always* be made that the manager may be fired "for cause."

Trap #17: The Preempted Powers Ploy. The bylaws may delegate policy-making powers to a professional management company that preempts the powers of the association's board of directors. This makes the board and the association powerless to deal with the management group.

Defense Against Preemption of Powers. A simple majority is all that is required to amend the bylaws of most enabling declarations, although some may require more. Any delegations of authority needed can be set forth in a simply worded amendment.

Trap #18: The "Straw Board" Gimmick. A builder may try to retain control of a condominium project long after he has turned it over to the association and its board of directors through what is called a "straw board" of directors. That is, the board of directors itself becomes nothing more than a subservient board manipulated by the builder. One modus operandi is for the builder to retain ownership of just over 50 percent of all the living units. This gives him control of the association and, through the association, the board.

Defense Against the "Straw Board." Be sure that there is a stipulation in the declaration to the effect that control of the board will be turned over to the unit owners *no matter what percentage of the total ownership they represent.*

Trap #19: The "Straw Board" Gimmick—Charlie McCarthy Variation. A builder may try to retain control of a project by selling a large number of units to Charlie McCarthys—puppet owners who are actually employees of the builder.

Defense Against the Puppet Board. The only way to fight this ploy is to discover it in time and never allow any of the builder's puppets to take over important jobs on the board of directors.

Trap #20: The "Straw Board" Gimmick—Phantom Owner Variation. A builder may try to control the board of directors of the association by writing in the declaration that third parties who are not unit owners may serve as members of the board of directors.

Defense Against Phantom Owner. Make sure that there is no such "third party" stipulation either in the declaration or in the bylaws of the condominium.

Trap #21: The "Straw Board" Gimmick—Zombi Voter Variation. A builder can try to write a clause permitting proxy voting during board-of-directors meetings and then manipulate the "zombi" voters himself.

Defense Against Zombi Voter. It is best to make sure there is no clause in the declaration or bylaws that permits proxy votes to be recorded at a board-of-directors meeting. The best associations allow only those board members present to vote and also have laws requiring a quorum large enough so that important decisions won't be made by only a handful of directors.

Trap #22: The "Designated Lender" Ploy. A builder may make a special deal with a "designated lender"—bank, individual, or group—in order to finance the construction of the condominium. This means that when you buy a unit in the condominium, you must take out your mortgage from the "designated lender" who financed the project.

Defense Against Pre-Picked Lender. Be sure you recognize this situation, if it exists. There is nothing wrong with dealing with the bank or lender the same as every other owner in the condominium, except that his mortgage rates must be comparable to those of other lenders in the area or to any accessible to you.

Trap #23: The "Implied Warranty" Gimmick. In some states the attorney general's office recognizes an "implied warranty of fitness and merchantability." In others, it does not. The "implied warranty" means that you will have no legal difficulty in holding a developer liable for faulty workmanship. In a state that does not recognize "implied warranty," you will not *be able to hold him liable for faulty workmanship.*

Defense Against the "Implied Warranty." The solution is a simple one. No matter what the situation, never depend on an "implied warranty." Make your builder give you an "express warranty" on faulty workmanship regarding roofing, walls, wiring, kitchen and bathroom cabinets, appliances, flooring, air-conditioning ducts, and other items you may be concerned about.

Trap #24: The Noncondominium Condominium.
Many living units are sold as condominiums but aren't
really condominiums at all. The typical planned unit
development (PUD) and the planned subdivision are not
really condominiums. As a member, you have an interest
in a separate property owned by a homeowners associa-
tion, but you do not, *usually, own an undivided interest*
in the entire development or subdivision. Therefore, you
are not a true condominium owner at all. If you do *own*
an undivided interest in the entire development or sub-
division, you are dealing with a condominium commu-
nity. Make sure you are right!

Defense Against the Phony Condominium. Make sure
you own undivided interest in all common property in
your project. It is a nasty surprise to find that you have
bought into what you thought was a condominium only to
find out that you haven't—or that you don't have any
interest at all in recreation facilities or grounds you
thought you owned. As a true condominium unit owner,
you *automatically* become a member of the organization,
with ownership of your unit and a responsibility for maintenance and operation of the common property.

... 7

How to Finance a Mortgage

FINANCING the purchase of the average condominium unit can be a nightmarish business—or it can be as easy as pie. If you already own a home and are moving from it because your children are grown up, married, and off on their own, then all you have to do is sell the house you live in and use the purchase money to buy your condominium unit outright. You may even have a bit of money left over.

However, if you do not own a home and have been renting all your life, you will have to take out a mortgage loan in order to purchase the condominium unit. The only exception, of course, is that you have enough cash on hand to purchase the unit outright.

The truth of the matter is that few families are able to pay cash for their homes—with the exception of the retiree or the "empty nest" couple. The typical homeowner borrows a large sum of money from a mortgage lender and pays him back on a monthly basis. A mortgage is quite simply the loan of a large sum of money, using the house —or condominium unit—as collateral and scheduled for repayment in small amounts over a period of twenty or thirty years.

WHERE DOES THE MONEY COME FROM?

Mortgage money is provided by savings banks—money put there by bank depositors, such as yourself—savings and loan associations, insurance companies, and mortgage bankers. Without the lender's authorization to use money from this pool of capital for long-term loans there would be very few older condominiums sold and very few newer condominiums built.

Legally, the mortgage is the lender's security that you, the buyer, will live up to your pledge to repay the loan. You, the buyer, are called the mortgagor; the lender is the mortgagee.

A mortgage loan resembles the ordinary type of loan you take out to buy an automobile. When you borrow to buy a car on credit, you sign a sales contract allowing the dealer, a finance company, or a bank to retain legal title to the car until you have paid the loan back. The car itself acts as security. Once the loan is repaid, the title is transferred to you.

When you take out a mortgage to buy a piece of real estate property, you use your home or condominium unit as security, or, in banking terms, collateral. The mortgage documents specify that if you fail to meet the repayment schedule, the lender will bring a foreclosure suit to recover the money.

But there is one essential difference between an automobile loan and a mortgage loan. It is in the way in which the interest is calculated.

Let's take a hypothetical case. Suppose you borrow $4,000 from your bank to purchase a car with a typical add-on installment loan. Your interest rate is 10 percent for a three-year repayment period. Say your monthly payments are $144.44 for 36 months. You repay a total of $5,200 by the time you own the car. Your financing costs amount to $1,200.

However, if you take out a $4,000 mortgage loan, instead of an auto loan, you may pay monthly installments of $129.07 for 36 months. Your total repayment is only $4,646.52 in three years—a difference of $553.48 ($6,200 − $4,646.52).

The reason for the difference is this: In arranging the car loan, the bank adds on the interest for all three years in advance. In other words, to get $4,000, you have to borrow $5,200—$1,200 extra ($4,000 × .10 × 3). In effect, the bank charges you interest on the *entire* amount of the loan for the three-year period. That accounts for the $144.44 per month payment.

By contrast, with a mortgage loan, interest is calculated only on the *unpaid balance* due after each monthly payment is made.

The Amortized Loan

Most mortgage loans today are the constant payment, self-liquidating type known technically as amortized loans. With the amortized loan, payments are the same each month over the years. A portion of every payment goes to pay the interest, and the rest goes to pay the principal. When the final payment is made, you own the property free and clear.

The amount of each monthly payment during the first years of the loan that goes to pay interest is quite large—about 93 percent of what you pay over the first seven years. Mortgages can even be set up to pay 100 percent interest in the first five years. The advantage of paying a heavy interest rate during the first years of the loan is obvious: you get a whopping tax deduction on your Internal Revenue Service form.

Every month you pay off any amount of the principal, you are only charged interest on the remainder of the principal. As you reduce the principal, you only owe interest on what remains. Your total monthly payment stays the same, but the proportion of interest and principal varies from month to month.

As you reduce the principal over the years, you increase the equity in the condo unit in reverse proportion. "Equity" is the proportion of the unit that belongs to you free of debt. In other words, your equity on a specific date includes the amount of principal that you have paid off plus whatever down payment you advanced to buy the condo unit. In addition, the value in money of any improvements you have made in the unit is also considered part of your equity. If the condo increases in value because of inflation, because of a prospering neighborhood, or for any other reason, your equity continues to grow.

When you sell your condo, your equity in it is equal to the difference between the amount of the mortgage you still owe and the total amount the buyer pays you for the property.

Inflation has contributed to one bad feature in today's money-lending market. Mortgage interest rates now hover around 10 or 11 percent (10.32 percent in January 1979). That means that with a twenty-five-year mortgage, you will actually be paying somewhere near *three and a half times* the actual sales price of your condominium unit! (25 × 10 percent = 250 percent + 100 percent of the price.)

THE GRADUATED-PAYMENT MORTGAGE

Bankers realize that saddling you with monthly payments in astronomical sums does not stimulate the sale of condo units. A new type of mortgage schedule has been worked out which differs from the conventional type in one important aspect: monthly payments are not equal for the full term of the mortgage loan. The payments at the beginning of the loan period are smaller, gradually increasing until the loan is paid off. Called the "graduated-payment mortgage," the new payment schedule lowers the initial costs for you when you are buying into your condo unit and need money to purchase furniture and household goods.

For example, on a conventional mortgage schedule you might pay $375 per month for a period of twenty-five years. The graduated-payment schedule might start out at $335 per month for five years, then rise to $350 per month for another five, and then go to $375 for five more, and so on until the mortgage is paid off.

The rationale behind this type of payment scheduling is an inflation-inspired one, of course. In theory, your income will increase as you continue to prosper, and you will have more money to pay your mortgage debt as you grow older and earn a larger salary.

DIFFERENT KINDS OF MORTGAGE LOANS

Although all mortgage loans are actually made by banks, savings and loan associations, insurance companies, and mortgage bankers, some of them may be guaranteed by agencies of the federal government. These include the so-called "VA loans" and "FHA loans." Most mortgage loans are conventional loans, *not* guaranteed by the government.

Veterans Administration Loans. Veterans Administration loans, also called GI loans, are loans guaranteed by the Veterans Administration. The government itself does not lend you the money, but the Veterans Administration does guarantee that the borrower will pay back the money. In other words, the VA simply insures the loan up to a certain amount, meaning that the lender will probably not suffer any loss in the event the home buyer fails to repay the loan.

The advantage for you as a buyer is that the VA loan permits the purchase of a condominium unit with little or no down payment. There are other advantages as well: a generally low rate of interest, a long period of amortization, and property appraisal by the Veterans Administration.

Veterans Administration inspectors are sticklers for construction and do not permit you to buy a piece of property they think is shoddily made or overpriced. Other rules and regulations—particularly those in some condominium bylaws—are not sanctioned by the Veterans Administration.

For that reason, there are few condominium sellers who will agree to finance through the Veterans Administration. If you are lucky enough to secure a Veterans Administration loan, you will know that you are getting a well-constructed and fairly priced piece of property.

Federal Housing Administration Loans. A mortgage loan insured by the Federal Housing Administration protects a lender from any losses if you fail to pay. After you make a small down payment for your property, you obtain a mortgage for the rest of the purchase price by borrowing the money from a bank, savings and loan association, mortgage company, insurance company, or other FHA-approved lender.

The loan is not made to you by the government; the amount of the loan is simply insured by the FHA. The Federal Housing Administration, like the Veterans Administration, does not lend money or build houses. Since FHA mortgage insurance protects the lender against loss on the mortgage, he can allow you more liberal mortgage terms for your condo than you might otherwise be able to get.

FHA insured loans usually require a lower down payment and have a longer maturity rate than conventional loans. To qualify for an FHA-insured loan, the property you are going to buy must meet FHA minimum standards. The Federal Housing Administration also requires certain useful financial regulations to protect you as a consumer.

Requirements for VA and FHA Financing. Both VA and FHA programs demand the following:

• All planned condominium construction for the project in which you are going to purchase a unit must be complete at the time of purchase.

• All down payments must be put into escrow accounts. These payments cannot be released to the builder until your unit is completed and title passes to you.

• The term of the mortgage may be as short as ten years and as long as thirty.

• The buyer's title must be free and clear, and the mortgage must be a first mortgage. The maximum limit of a VA and FHA mortgage is set at a specific amount. Because prices continue to rise with inflation, the limit will vary from year to year. And the limit can also be changed by the VA or FHA at any time. You can always contact your bank to find out what the present limit is.

• At least 80 percent of the condominium units in a project must have been sold before the Federal Housing Administration or Veterans Administration will guarantee any buyer's mortgage.

• The FHA also requires certain agreements from the builder covering vital aspects of condominium life.

For example, the condo builder must show evidence that the project has been built with compliance to all zoning laws.

He must provide a surety bond against latent defects in the construction equal to 2.5 percent of your total mortgage.

He must show a regulatory agreement providing for cash reserves for maintenance and replacement of worn-out roofs, equipment, etc.

He must show how assessments and collections for maintenance and upkeep are made, how defaults will be handled, how upkeep, record-keeping, and reporting are accomplished.

He must also prevent remodeling or changes in the condominium without Federal Housing Administration approval.

• The FHA will not insure a loan if the condominium you are going to move into has a lease-back clause in its bylaws. It stipulates that you as condominium unit owner must hold an *undivided interest* in *all common property,* among which are all recreational features. Therefore, since you "own" these areas, you cannot be forced to "lease" them from the owner.

• Nor will the FHA insure a loan if the condominium allows family units to be rented for transient or hotel purposes. You as an owner, however, do have the right to lease or rent your unit to someone else for residential purposes. The "transient or hotel" clause is an important one issued by the Federal Housing Administration in order to protect you from moving into a nonresidential type of building.

• The most important consideration that the Federal Housing Administration does not approve is "first refusal." The "first refusal" clause is written into some condominium contracts in order to control all buyers who might come into the project. As a seller, you are required to offer your unit first to the condominium homeowners association rather than the buyer of your choice. The clause effectively prevents you from selling to whomever you wish. By limiting insurance only to those condominiums that allow you free choice in determining who will buy and occupy your unit after you leave, the FHA protects you from the financially troublesome situation of being unable to sell to an "unapproved" buyer.

Thus, the Federal Housing Administration and the Veterans Administration demand certain particulars from the condominium builder before either will agree to insure a loan you might take out to buy a unit in such a property. Because their guidelines are so strict, and because many condominiums do not adhere to the principles they espouse, you will find that you are not able to get VA- or FHA-guaranteed loans except for a very few projects.

In fact, not more than 5 percent of all condominium loans are VA- or FHA-insured. Nevertheless, government-insured loans are cheaper, more easily paid, and protect you from construction defects and management abuses.

Incidentally, you are allowed to assume someone else's Veterans Administration loan with its advantageous interest rates even if you are not a veteran yourself.

Conventional Mortgage Loans. Almost all condominium loans are conventional mortgage loans made between two parties: the borrower (you) and the lender (the bank). No government guarantee backs the lender if you default. At the same time, the lender is free to charge you the going rate of interest, no matter how high it is. He also can decide what construction standards are required in the condominium you want to buy. He can also determine if you qualify as a buyer.

Because he is not dependent on the VA or FHA to insure his loan, he has a great deal more flexibility to adapt to the ever-changing financial and housing markets.

Generally speaking, a savings and loan association requires a smaller down payment on a conventional mortgage loan than other lenders, but you are likely to be charged a slightly higher interest rate. The figures vary from one part of the country to another and are also subject to the fluctuations of the money market.

You may be able to get financing for 75 percent of your condo unit from one lender, whereas another might go as high as 90 percent. That means if you want to buy a $50,000 condo unit, the first lender would demand $12,500 in cash, with the rest as the mortgage loan, whereas the second would demand only $5,000, and lend you the balance of $45,000.

One lender may set a twenty-year mortgage term; another may set a twenty-five-year term. Most conventional mortgages now run from twenty-five to thirty-five years. It is important for you to shop around for a loan. If you don't get a loan on the first try, look around some more. The mortgage money picture changes rapidly from day to day. A lender who turned you down a few weeks ago may reverse himself if you approach him again.

How Much Will the Bank Lend You?

Now for the nitty-gritty. Do you, in fact, make enough money so that a lender will find you a positive prospect for a mortgage loan to finance the condo purchase you want to make?

Lenders vary from place to place and from time to time, but currently the climate is such that a lender will allow you loan money on either of two conditions:

• If your loan payments *and* maintenance fees add up to no more than 25 percent of your gross income.

• If your total monthly obligations—loan payments and maintenance fees and utilities, *plus* auto payments, alimony, if any, and so on—total no more than one-third of your gross income.

For example, if your monthly obligations in the first instance total, say, $1,000 before deductions, you should be earning $48,000 a year ($1,000 × 12 months × 4). If your monthly household outgo *plus* time payments total, say, $1,600 before deductions, you should also be earning $48,000.

Incidentally, the banking business has at last discovered the fact that more than half the wives in the country are a part of the working force and that many of them do not intend to quit work at a whim. Most lenders now allow you to include *both incomes* of a married couple in the calculations above.

Assuming an Existing Mortgage

Let's suppose you are interested in buying a condominium unit from someone who has not yet paid off his mortgage loan. Part of the deal is that he allows you to take over his existing mortgage, after you have paid him a certain amount in cash—an amount equal to his equity and whatever profit is feasible.

There is one special advantage for you. The interest rate on his mortgage is probably quite a bit lower than the going rate now at the time of your purchase. For example, many old mortgages now carry 6 to 9 percent interest rates, compared with 10 or 11 percent at the present time.

The assumption of an existing mortgage will cut down on your closing costs, because of the minimum of paperwork. You do, however, have to pay a small fee for recording the deed and modifying the contract.

You cannot always get such a deal, however. Some mortgages contain a clause preventing such takeovers by requiring full payment of the mortgage in the event of sale. Other mortgages include a clause stating that the mortgage may be assumed—but only at the going interest rate at the time of assumption.

If the original mortgage carries an 8 percent interest rate, you might have to pay a higher rate—say, 10 percent —if you assume the mortgage. The reason for such a clause is obvious: lenders do not want to continue an 8 percent mortgage when the current interest rate is much higher.

There is one large problem with assuming an existing mortgage. Suppose you bought a $50,000 condominium ten years ago, paying $10,000 down, and taking out a $40,000 mortgage. Since the time you moved in, you have reduced the mortgage to $25,000. Now you want to sell the condo. The going price is $70,000, as against your original $50,000. You have built equity in the condominium through the mortgage in the amount of $15,000. With the mortgage reduced to $25,000, the buyer will have to put up $45,000 cash to buy the unit with the existing mortgage! Who has that kind of money today? Or even if he has it, who wants to tie it all up in the condominium?

USING A SECOND MORTGAGE

The *second mortgage* is a type of loan that can help a buyer pick up an attractive existing mortgage.

Suppose, continuing the above situation, you found a buyer who would pay you $70,000 for the condo and assume your $25,000 mortgage. Of the $45,000 required, he has only $20,000 in cash. In short, he needs $25,000 to go through with the purchase.

You agree to grant the buyer a second mortgage to cover the $25,000. That amount is to be repaid in five years; it is called a second mortgage, because it is taken out in addition to the original, or first, mortgage.

Many times a builder will take a second mortgage to make up the difference between the down payment required for purchase and the amount of cash the buyer has in hand. Most lenders will give second mortgages.

There are three types of second mortgages, generally speaking: the amortizing mortgage, the "balloon" mortgage, and the graduated payment mortgage.

The *amortizing second mortgage* is scheduled for repayment exactly like a regular mortgage, except that the repayment period usually is much shorter.

The *"balloon" mortgage* works a little differently. Monthly payments at first are a great deal lower than they would be with a fully amortized loan—about half, in fact. At the end of the full five years, your mortgage would be only about one-third paid off. *Then* you would have to come up with the total amount of the remaining portion of the loan—called the "balloon" because it balloons at the end of the schedule.

The *graduated payment mortgage* is similar to the balloon mortgage, except that the payments are graduated more steadily and there is no balloon at the end of the schedule—just larger and larger payments.

The last two types of second mortgages are the obvious and welcome solution to a situation where you cannot afford the property if you have to make high monthly payments on a fully amortizing five-year second mortgage.

WHAT ARE POINTS?

When you are dealing with banks and lending institutions you may come across the use of a strange term that does not seem to make sense to you: For example, "That will be a three-point charge."

Actually a "point," or "points," since the word is usually used in the plural, is used in discussing fees for the placement of a mortgage with a lender. A point is simply 1 percent of the total amount of the mortgage.

For example, placement of a $35,000 mortgage at two points would signify a charge of $700.

Points are generally charged to the seller and paid by him. However, if the seller is going to have to pay a substantial sum in points to arrange the mortgage, he is apt to increase the price of the house to cover the added expense.

Any way you look at it, you are probably going to be the one to wind up paying the fee.

You won't run across mention of points except in times of extremely tight money, when lending institutions do not have large amounts of money to advance to make mortgage fees.

WHAT IS A PREPAYMENT CLAUSE?

A prepayment clause in a mortgage allows you to pay off part or all of the principal earlier than the schedule calls for. Many conventional mortgages do not allow you to pay off your mortgage in advance of its time of closing; or if they do, they charge you a stiff penalty. The reason is a simple one: the lender loses interest charges —and that is the reason he lends you the money in the first place.

Veterans Administration mortgages allow you to prepay without penalty. Federal Housing Administration mortgages let you prepay up to 45 percent of the principal in any one year without penalty.

WHAT IS AN OPEN-END CLAUSE?

An open-end clause permits you to refinance your loan without paying any new financing charges. This type of loan can come in handy if you want to refinance so you can send one of your children to college.

HOW MUCH ARE CLOSING COSTS?

Once you arrange financing for your condominium unit you are ready to take the final step—"settlement," or, as it is usually called, "closing."

Closing is the time the buyer and seller exchange documents and payments, and ownership passes from one to the other. And in closing the deal, "closing costs" are paid. This term covers a half-dozen or more costs that have to be paid—in cash—when you take title to your condo property.

The term "closing costs" refers to all charges paid for obtaining the mortgage loan and transferring the title of the condominium unit. While the distribution of closing cost items may be agreed to in the contract of purchase, all or a significant part of the closing costs are paid by you, the buyer.

Among the items which you are required to pay for are the following:

- title search
- title insurance
- attorney fees
- survey
- credit report
- appraisal fee
- recording fee
- state and/or local transfer taxes
- lender's origination fee
- mortgage-processing charge
- taxes and insurance

Title insurance. It is required by most lenders for you to purchase what is known as "mortgage title insurance." The insurance protects the lender if your ownership right to the property ever comes into dispute. The policy covers the full amount of the mortgage principal. At the payment of the mortgage, the policy terminates. Premiums vary. You can also purchase "owner's title insurance" to give you the same protection you are giving the lender.

Attorney fees are included in the closing costs. Charges vary, but if you have received legal advice throughout the negotiations, you may pay from $50 to $200 or more.

Credit report is a check on your credit rating. The fee is anywhere from $5 to $15 or more. If you are a new resident and your credit references are at some distant place, the fee may be higher.

The *appraisal fee* is generally from $20 to $50, but may be higher, depending on local practice. It refers to the appraisal ordered by the lender when you are negotiating the loan.

Mortgage-processing charges may be called a mortgage service fee, initial service fee, brokerage fee, origination fee, or some other name. By paying it, you reimburse the lender for the paperwork necessary at the closing. The fee is usually about 1 percent of the mortgage, but in some areas, it is even higher than that.

Taxes and insurance. With Veterans Administration or Federal Housing Administration loans, escrow payments are required for property taxes and fire and hazard insurance. The maximum prepayment is one calendar year. If you purchased in the fall, you would only pay for three months' taxes and insurance.

...8

Condominium Paper Chase

YOU may have heard that buying a condominium is pretty much like buying a traditional single-family house. The two transactions involve signing a sales contract, arranging a mortgage loan, and signing a lot of papers at the closing.

But there are important differences.

In addition to the traditional documents required in the purchase of an ordinary house, you'll be required to understand a number of documents that are more or less restricted to buying a condominium. Naturally, the responsibility for these legal documents should of necessity rest with a qualified lawyer. Even so, you should know exactly what the documents are and what they refer to in general.

Here are the main documents that you will be facing, roughly in the order you will encounter them:

- Nonbinding reservation
- Purchase and sales agreement
- Enabling declaration
- Association bylaws
- House rules
- Other documents

NONBINDING RESERVATION

This document is not necessary for every transaction, but is handy to use when you want to reserve a particular unit in a condominium at a given price to hold it for a specified period of time.

Known as "earnest money," the deposit necessary to reserve your unit can be as little as $50 or so. The nonbinding reservation is used by a builder who has an agreement with a lender requiring the builder to secure a specific number of tentative acceptances for units before advancing the money with which to begin construction.

Even if the project falls through, your reservation deposit is normally refundable, but it's always a good idea to have this stated in your receipt.

PURCHASE AND SALES AGREEMENT

The purchase and sales agreement is a sales contract for the particular unit in the condominium you want to buy. This document is known by a number of names, including subscription and purchase agreement, conditional sales contract, or simply purchase agreement.

As a sales agreement, it is similar to the type you would sign in buying any kind of residential real estate. Essentially, it is the contract that shows you have agreed to purchase a piece of property for a specified sum of money.

• First of all, the document identifies the unit you're buying, with a clear description of its size, shape, and properties. It also mentions the individual interest in the common condominium property attached to the unit.

• It identifies you as the buyer and the builder or salesperson as the seller.

• It specifies the amount of the purchase and contains

all other essential financial facts about the transaction.

• It mentions the amount of the down payment required.

• It specifies the cooling-off period—usually at least ten days—in which you can back out of the deal if you wish without losing either the down payment or the "earnest money" required. A down payment on a condo unit is usually a substantial sum. You will be safer if you specify that the money be held in escrow for you until the condominium is completed.

• The document also contains a clause saying that by signing you acknowledge receiving and accepting all "organizational" documents. If the contract doesn't give you the right to withdraw within a certain period, don't sign until you have received the condominium documents and have studied them carefully—with the assistance of a lawyer. These documents usually include the enabling declaration, association bylaws, and house rules, if any.

Checklist for Purchase and Sales Contract:

1. First of all, be sure to have a lawyer look over the agreement and discuss any features that you do not fully understand. Also, ask the lawyer if he thinks the agreement is acceptable or not.

2. Find out whether or not the declaration date of the project has been specifically defined in the contract. This date is the day the project officially becomes a condominium; it should be set forth in writing.

3. If you are going to put a deposit on a particular unit, be sure the deposit will be placed in an escrow account for your protection. Also, request that the escrow account bear interest for you.

4. In addition, you should make sure that whatever deposit or "earnest money" you put down to reserve a

unit temporarily will be returned to you upon your request in the event that the sale falls through for any reason whatsoever.

5. Be sure that return of your deposit is guaranteed in writing if a specific number of units in the condo should fail to be built by a certain date. If the development fails to sell enough units to become a condo, you should get back every cent you have advanced.

6. If not enough units have been sold to make the condo project officially a condominium, be sure you have the right to rent the unit rather than buy it. This is particularly important if you have made plans to move from your own present place of residence.

7. If you are forced into a rental situation because there are not yet enough condo units sold to finish the project, be sure that the rental costs will be applied to the anticipated condo purchase price.

8. Make sure the builder promises not to use your deposit money for any construction purpose until the condominium has sold a satisfactory number of units.

9. Find out what specific arrangements have been made by the builder for long-term financing of the condominium.

10. Be sure that all financial commitments to which you will be bound have been clearly spelled out and are understood beforehand. These obligations include the following:

- *Nonbinding reservation deposit*
- *Down payment*
- *Initial cash payments.* These include the first down payments on the condominium unit.
- *Mortgage payments.* Be sure you understand the terms of the mortgage—specifically the amount of interest you will be paying, the amount of the principal, and

any added charges that might be lumped in with the carrying charges.

• *Real estate taxes.* Find out whether or not your real estate taxes are included in with the mortgage payments. It is an unpleasant surprise to discover that you owe another two thousand dollars in real estate taxes after your mortgage is paid for the year.

• *Maintenance fee.* Be sure you understand thoroughly exactly what you are obligated to pay for in your maintenance fee and what you get out of it. Maintenance fees, operating fees, and utilities costs should be clearly defined.

THE ENABLING DECLARATION

The enabling declaration may also be called the master deed, the declaration of conditions, covenants and restrictions, or the plan of condominium ownership.

Whatever it is called, it is the legal instrument that, when recorded, converts a previous owner's property into a number of single ownerships and extends the state's condominium laws to the project. It corresponds to an ordinary single-house deed.

The document essentially *enables* the condominium to come into existence by legally establishing a condominium "regime." It also contains conditions, covenants, and restrictions, which become the constitutional law of the condominium once the declaration is recorded.

It arranges for the establishment of a homeowners association to be governed by a board of directors. It confers upon the directors the power to administer and regulate the common condominium property, including the authority to provide professional management. It enables them to enforce restrictions that are binding on all property owners.

In addition, the declaration also gives the association the authority to assess and collect sufficient money to physically maintain the common property and to maintain the financial stability of the condo. It provides for legal enforcement of unpaid monthly charges or special assessments in the form of a lien against an individual unit estate.

If you ignore a covenant—an agreement to do or not do something—you can become liable for damages and corrective action. Failure to pay an assessment can subject you to a penalty that can range all the way up to the calling of your mortgage.

The declaration also describes the individual units and any common property, such as parking spaces, that particular owners can use exclusively. It specifies what arrangements have been made for hazard and liability insurance on the condominium's common property. The policy should name both the board and each unit owner as insureds.

The document also spells out what percentage of the common property you will own jointly with the other owners. This proportion will determine what share of the maintenance charges will be allocated to you, what proportion of the condominium's real estate taxes you will be expected to bear, and, if your association votes are weighted, how many votes you will have in condo affairs.

Checklist for Enabling Declaration. In checking over the enabling declaration, you should obtain information on all these following subjects in their entirety:

1. Be sure that there is a clear-cut distinction between the property you own in your unit and the property you

own in common with all the other unit owners. In the case of a recreational facility, you should find out exactly how many people you are going to share it with and how much your monthly maintenance fees are going to be to pay for it.

2. Make sure you understand exactly what your percentage of ownership of the common property is. It will determine the amount of your monthly maintenance fee. Here's the way percentage of ownership is determined in one hypothetical case:

Unit	Initial Sale Price	Percentage of Ownership
1	$80,000	16%
2	$100,000	20
3	$110,000	22
4	$120,000	24
5	$90,000	18
	$500,000	100%

For example, Unit 1 has an initial sale price of $80,000, which is 16 percent of the total sale price of $500,000.

$$\text{Unit 1} = \frac{\$80,000 \text{ (initial sale price)}}{\$500,000 \text{ (total sales price)}} = 16\%$$

Incidentally, at the time of the purchase of the condominium unit, the recorded percentages are established by law, and they remain the same even if the unsold units eventually sell for more or for less than was originally declared.

Suppose all five units were sold at the prices indicated,

except for Unit 4. The prospective buyer for Unit 4 was unable to consummate the sale, and for reasons of market values no other buyer would be found for a half year. At that point the builder reduced the price to $105,000. Unit 4's owner would still command 24 percent of the total ownership, in spite of the fact that he did not actually pay 24 percent of the total aggregate cost.

3. Find out the number of votes you as owner of your unit are entitled to cast in meetings of the association. Most condominiums have a one-man one-vote rule, but not all of them do. In some condominiums where certain owners own twice or three times as much as others, an owner may be allocated two votes, or even three. Or the number may be 78 (of 1,000).

4. Be sure you know the exact amount you will be assessed for maintenance and operation of the common properties. Make the salesperson sit down with you and detail the estimated annual and monthly assessments for maintenance, rubbish removal, reserve assessments for the entire development and for your own unit. Watch out if the amount seems abnormally low—it can only mean that it will rise precipitately later on.

5. Check on the amount of real estate tax that is assessed against the unit you are going to buy. Don't forget that you will be paying real estate taxes not only on your individual unit—and pay that in full—but also for all the common condominium property you co-own with all the other owners—and pay that in proportion to your percentage of ownership.

6. Find out the amount of money you can borrow on your unit and your percentage of the common area if you wanted to take out a loan on your property. This is an important fact that you should know; you may not need the money now, but you might in the future.

7. Make sure there is no language in the declaration that allows for unit ratios to *change* at some future date. Unit ratios are set at the time of the declaration and should never alter. A change in your percentage of ownership would adversely affect the undivided interest in the condominium common property that is coupled to your unit.

8. Find out if the condominium property will be retained by the builder or by a third party rather than deeded over to the unit owners. Such a condominium is called a "leasehold condominium." If yours is a leasehold condo, you must find out exactly the terms and restrictions of the lease, since you will have no control over the leaseheld property. Get help from a lawyer or disinterested real estate agent.

9. Be sure that the builder offers warranties on the facilities of the building and on the appliances in your unit. Most equipment, appliances, and materials are warranteed for a certain period of time in any new construction. This helps protect you as a new unit owner from liability for obvious construction faults. In older buildings, make the seller warrantee central facilities such as wiring, plumbing, heating system, and roofing for at least a year.

10. Check out the "use description" of the building. In other words, make sure the zoning won't permit some business enterprise such as a fast-food franchise to move in, bringing crowds, noise, and traffic problems. The building should be restricted to residential use.

11. Make sure that the declaration restricts the right to partition individual units. Partitioning could mean increasing the number of residents in the condominium.

12. If more units and facilities are to be built in the future, make sure that the declaration gives the association authority to acquire and to hold units and any addi-

tional property and facilities built within the boundaries of the condominium property.

ASSOCIATION BYLAWS

To satisfy the requirement of the law, it is necessary for the association bylaws of the condominium to be recorded along with the enabling declaration. Sometimes called the secondary laws of the condominium, these bylaws cover all the rules and regulations that apply to the condominium, including the establishment of the owners board of directors and guidelines by which they must rule. Whereas the declaration establishes the authority to form the association, the bylaws govern the way in which it is run.

All present or future owners, tenants, future tenants, or their employees, or any other person who might use the facilities of the project are subject to the regulations set forth in the bylaws.

Either the declaration or the bylaws should contain a covenant that the mere acquisition or rental of any of the family units of the project, or the mere act of occupancy of any of those units, has the effect of signifying that the bylaws are accepted, ratified, and will be complied with.

Generally speaking, the bylaws establish a plan for the governing of the condominium and usually include the following main points:

• *The administration of the condominium.* The bylaws usually state that the condominium will be operated by the builder until the first meeting of the association of homeowners. At that time, the association will elect its board of directors, which will take over the government of the condominium.

• *Owner responsibilities.* The bylaws spell out the responsibilities of each owner with regard to elections and special meetings. It states what constitutes a majority of owners and a quorum for doing business, method of voting, use of proxies, removal of any undesirable board member, and the manner in which the bylaws can be amended. Usually, a simple majority of votes of the association members can amend the bylaws. However, some condominium organizations require a two-thirds majority.

• *The responsibility of the board of directors and the officers of the association.* The bylaws authorize the board and officers to carry out the conditions, covenants, and restrictions set forth in the declaration. It cites the number, qualifications, powers, duties, and term of office of officers and directors. The bylaws also set forth the rules for conducting meetings: the order of business, quorum, proxies, and number of votes required to resolve an issue.

More specifically, the bylaws contain the following details establishing the rights and responsibilities of the owners:

• Collection of monthly dues and special assessments, including the enforcement of a lien for unpaid amounts
• Notice to lenders of unpaid assessments
• Use and maintenance of common property
• Establishment of an operating budget including general operating reserve and reserve for replacement of common elements
• Provision for professional management, if necessary
• Right of entry and rules of conduct with respect to the common areas
• Fire and other hazard insurance (*not* including fire and hazard insurance on your own unit)
• General liability insurance (*not* including your own liability)
• Use of the dwelling units for residential purposes and

rules of conduct which would be necessary to preserve the aesthetic appearance of the development and promote harmony among the users
• Compliance with state laws

CHECKLIST FOR BYLAWS

Some of the salient points to check carefully in studying the bylaws are the following:

1. Make sure there are provisions for changing the bylaws, including the percentage of the vote needed to make the changes permanent.

2. Make sure there are provisions in the bylaws for settling disputes among owners.

3. Be sure there is a clear-cut statement of the way in which the power of the builder will be turned over to the association of homeowners.

4. Be sure that the machinery of the homeowners association is clearly spelled out.

5. Check for a method for establishing regulation over the common property of the condominium.

6. Look for adequate machinery for deciding maintenance and building repair questions.

7. There should be a statement in the bylaws binding all owners of units to obey the association's bylaws, and there should be a means of enforcing compliance with the bylaws.

8. The procedure for calling and running meetings of the homeowners association should be stated clearly in writing.

9. There should be an explanation of the arrangements the builder has made to assure quality upkeep in the condominium once he has turned it over to the owners. Be sure these arrangements are adequate.

10. Make sure you are satisfied that the insurance is

adequate for the common property of the condominium —fire, theft, liability.

HOUSE RULES

Many condominiums do not have so-called "house rules." Others call them "rules and regulations." Still others include these items in the bylaws. Nevertheless, there should be provision somewhere for rules and regulations for unit owners.

Even what you do in the privacy of your own unit will probably be subject to some restrictions. Some house rules bar residents who have pets or even children under a specified age. Others may declare how late and how loud you may play your stereo.

The most important thing about such house rules is that you read them, understand what they mean, and decide that you can abide by them.

Common house rules found in a typical list of rules and regulations include the following:

• Public passageways, hallways, elevators, and stairways shall not be obstructed or used for any purpose other than for ingress or egress from the condominium units and to the common areas in the condominium.

• Bicycles, baby carriages, scooters, or similar vehicles shall not be placed in or allowed to stand in the public areas within the common elements.

• Clothing items, umbrellas, umbrella stands, clothes racks, and toys shall not be placed in the hallways outside the condominium unit entrances or service doors or in any other common areas.

• No garbage cans, supplies, milk containers, or other articles shall be placed in passageways, hallways, or the stairways and stairway landings.

• Linens, clothing, draperies, swimwear, rugs, mops, or laundry shall not be shaken or hung from any exposed part of the building.

• Children shall not be permitted to play or loiter in the lobby, hallways, stairways, elevators, walkways, driveways, parking areas, or any other common areas.

• No common areas of the condominium shall be decorated or furnished by any individual owner or group of owners in any manner, except with the written approval of the board of directors.

• Owners shall park only in the owned or leased parking spaces.

• Horns should not be used or blown while cars are parked or standing in driveways and/or parking area. Racing engines or loud exhausts should be avoided.

• Elevator service shall not be delayed for the sake of conversation by using the HOLD button or the STOP switch.

• No resident may make or permit any disturbing noise in the building or permit anything to be done to interfere with the rights, comfort, or convenience of other residents.

• Pets shall be on a leash at all times while in the common areas of the condominium.

• Nothing shall be swept, poured, tossed, or shaken from the terraces.

• Owners, lessees, or guests shall not be permitted to directly give orders or direction to any building staff employee.

• All recreational facilities are restricted to the use of owners, lessees, their families, and registered guests.

• There shall be no ball playing, running, shouting, or excessive noise in the pool area or elsewhere on condominium property.

OTHER DOCUMENTS

Occasionally there will be other documents involved in the transaction that pertain not only to the purchase of your individual unit, but affect the condominium as a whole and you as a co-owner.

One of the most important of these papers is the maintenance budget mentioned in Chapter Ten and with it a schedule of monthly assessments.

In addition, there may be a contract with a management firm to run the condominium. Look it over. The condo may pay the manager too much money. Or it may shortchange the manager—in which case you'll be in for trouble in the form of truncated or grudging service.

There may be a warranty for the basic components in the condominium—wiring, plumbing, heating, and air-conditioning equipment.

Some condominiums issue separate deeds to each owner of a unit. Others do not. The wording of the declaration may contain your legal ownership of your unit. It may not.

Obviously, you may need professional help in the analysis of these documents. Don't get just any lawyer; get a real estate lawyer who is familiar with condominiums.

You can always go to your local bar association or real estate board for names. The charges may be anywhere from $50 to $200 or more for giving you advice on your move, but that isn't much when you consider the amount you are going to spend on the transaction itself.

...9

Who Buys a Condo and Why– Is It for You?

CERTAIN types of living appeal to certain groups of people. Apartments have always appealed to single people who do not have families. Suburban homes have always appealed to families if they can afford them. Second homes have always appealed to recreation-minded people with enough money to indulge themselves.

Who is it, actually, who chooses to live in the condominium, with its rather special lifestyle?

A survey of condominium owners between the ages of thirty and thirty-nine published recently by the Urban Land Institute reveals some interesting findings:

• Most of the condominium owners surveyed were married.

• Of those who weren't married, more than twice as many owned condominiums in California than owned them in the East or South.

Findings from the Urban Land Institute survey, answers to questions posed to condominium owners, and extensive interviews with people living in townhouses and high-rise condos form a valuable picture of the average condominium owner—and help to point out what the real appeal of the condominium is to those who have become owners.

FIRST, THE GOOD NEWS. . . .

Three out of four condominium owners questioned in the Urban Land Institute survey said that they found the lifestyle satisfactory or better than satisfactory. Only one out of four thought there might be a better way of life.

The ratio of those interviewed independently adhered closely to the findings of the survey. Indeed, the over-all findings of the interviews reported here confirmed the original study's results.

Freedom from Maintenance. The main reason most people listed for liking condominium life was the lack of home repair and maintenance—namely, that there was no need for a great deal of time-consuming and energy-vitiating chores on the property.

One respondent said that he had spent many hours of each weekend repairing the home he owned prior to buying a condo, trying to keep it up so it wouldn't deteriorate. Now, since he had moved into a condominium, he was able to spend his time in more enjoyable enterprises—recreation, family matters, and individual hobbies.

Another pointed out that he did not know a thing about home repair and maintenance, and for that reason he had always rented space in apartments so he wouldn't be confronted with a home repair crisis which would demonstrate his ineptitude with tools. In a condominium he was protected from this eventuality—and in addition he could take advantage of all the pluses that ownership of property afforded him.

Still another—this one a housewife—said that life in a condominium had improved her marriage to a considerable degree. Her husband, not essentially a man with a flair for tools and carpentry, had almost been on the verge of emotional collapse trying to accomplish all the chores he was forced to undertake in their house. Since going condo, he had become a better spouse in every way.

As for the general feeling of freedom from all types of cares, the wife of a truck driver had this to say: "I dearly love our new home and am happier here than in any other place I've lived. For anyone whose family has matured and left the nest this is ideal living."

More Value for Your Money. The second most important reason condominium owners listed for liking the life was that they got a lot more value out of their money in a condominium than in a house.

Most condominium units are cheaper than those of equivalent-sized detached houses. A two-bedroom condominium, typically, may cost 15 to 20 percent less than a two-bedroom home. Of course, maintenance charges must be added to the initial cost of the condominium to give a fair figure, but maintenance costs for an individual home are also high.

Superior Investment Advantages. The third reason most owners liked the condominium was its superior investment advantages—in other words, they felt that owning their own property afforded them an excellent financial investment. As a piece of real estate, the condominium became, in addition, an inflation hedge which helped appreciate their total worth as inflation whittled down their dollar earnings.

Owning a living unit gave them a chance to invest in it, rather than simply pay a rental fee each month for the temporary use of the property. Since they owned the condo unit, it became theirs to sell at a later date when they wanted to move. And while they were living in it, they were building equity which they could later take with them on sale of the unit.

One owner pointed out that he had always considered

owning real estate a rich man's game, but, since buying his condominium unit, he realized it was a good way for a middle-income man to enjoy the advantages of owning property and to enjoy also the advantages afforded property owners by property deductions allowed by the Internal Revenue Service.

Another, who had never invested in stocks or bonds, said ownership of a condominium unit had made him an investor for the first time in his life, and he liked the feeling of independence and financial security it gave him.

Proximity of Neighbors. Most condominium owners liked the fact that they were closer to their neighbors than they would be in a private home. They cited this increased human relationship with people around them as a desirable feature of condominium life.

An auditor's wife in a town house condo said, "The closeness of homes creates a closer feeling among neighbors."

"Our neighbors are young and friendly and we have much in common," a young engineer commented. "For this reason our block has a fantastic community spirit that has made life here very enjoyable."

One woman who had always lived in a suburban environment said she was much happier in her condominium. She felt that the proximity of people was a very definite plus in her lifestyle. During her youth she had been home when her father had a heart attack in the house. She had telephoned for the police and ambulance, but had suffered a great deal of emotional turmoil before either arrived. Even though her father did pull through his attack, she had never forgotten the traumatic experience. She felt that neighbors close by were necessary for her sense of security.

Better Recreational Facilities. Almost as important as the proximity of neighbors was the easy access to recreational facilities in the typical condominium. Almost everyone questioned remarked on this particular facet of condo life.

Not only conventional facilities like swimming pools and tennis courts were cited, but bowling alleys as well, squash courts, handball courts, cinder paths, bicycle lanes, gymnasium facilities, and countless other kinds of recreation.

"Recreation is important in our hyped-up modern life," one advertising executive said. "You've got to take care of the body so it won't let you down. The Romans were good ad copywriters. One of them, Juvenal, wrote: *Mens sana in corpore sano.* (A healthy mind in a healthy body.) That makes good sense."

Of all the types of recreation available in condominium facilities, the swimming pool was the one most often mentioned. Many people who had become swimming and suntan addicts had never before had access to private swimming pools. They loved the healthful aspects of swimming—not only for its physical effects but for its social aspects as well.

Good Security Measures. It is not surprising that in these days of increasing crime in the cities and suburbs the subject of security should be important to the condominium owner. Most condominiums hire their own security guards and are not dependent on the public police—although, of course, in cases of crime, the public force is always summoned.

Nevertheless, security—freedom from vandalism, particularly, as well as from theft and violence—is a very important element in the ideal condo environment.

One respondent said that he now carried money in his

wallet once again when he went out. When he had lived in a city apartment, he had felt forced to stuff his money and credit cards into a money belt.

Another with a teenage daughter said she finally felt as if she did not have to worry about the fact that her daughter had to take a bus to and from school every day.

Architectural Design. One out of four people thought the designs of the condominium structures were good—particularly town houses and detached houses.

"The well-designed condominium town house offers far more reasonable living than a single-family home," one financial analyst said. "We have a large eat-in kitchen, a den with fireplace, a recreation room, and plenty of storage."

One owner said that he lived in a remodeled mansion in an exclusive suburb. The house, built over a century ago, had been refurbished and then remodeled for condominium units. He said he felt like an English aristocrat living in a country home—not a bad feeling when he considered the relatively small amount of money it cost him.

. . . AND NOW FOR THE BAD NEWS

As important in a study of a lifestyle as the popular aspects are the unpopular aspects. And a look at these can afford a good idea of the kinds of people who do not like the general lifestyle of the condominium.

For about every three who liked condos, there was one who did not especially like it—although many of these continued to live in the condominium atmosphere in spite of its drawbacks.

Overcrowding. As a counterbalance to those who liked the intimate, friendly, close-to-people environment, there were those who disliked it almost as vehemently.

Overcrowding gave many of them the feeling of claustrophobia. A federal employee in his twenties said, "Our builder has a good product but he's packed too many people into this area." A young biologist echoed the complaint by adding, "The most serious problem here is overcrowding. Planning for this development was done strictly to maximize density and profits."

In many cases the condo owners were living in a complex where there were ten condominium units to an acre —and they thought that the number was too many for town house designs.

True. Most experts on condos agree that there should be only about seven or eight units to an acre. Naturally, that does not include high-rises, which must be considered generally high-density structures equivalent to apartment buildings.

Most condominium owners considered low-density condos "better" than high-density condos. Small projects seemed to get higher marks than large projects; short rows were liked more than long rows of town houses.

It is obvious that the proximity of people can be good for one person and bad for another.

Lack of Privacy. For the person who likes a lot of people around him, there is his opposite number who *doesn't.* People create noise. There are people who do not like noise, even if modified.

Overcrowding and lack of privacy got bad marks from about one out of every four condominium owners. An electrical engineer in a town house commented, "Lack of privacy is the biggest drawback for us. Walls should be more soundproof, backyards should be enclosed, parking should be away from dwellings."

Many of these lovers of privacy said they later bought

units with enclosed patios and fenced-in areas with greater privacy and quiet available.

Pet Control. Although some condominium associations don't allow pets of any kind, others do. It is advisable for anyone purchasing a condo to check into the management's pet-control rules, if any, before making a final decision.

One of the negative factors commonly encountered in condominium living is the lack of control of pets—usually dogs. Cats are not particularly despised. However, the dog—man's best friend!—comes in for a great deal of animosity.

For one thing, a large healthy dog is a joy to his owner, but he is not a joy to a total stranger, or even to a friendly neighbor. In some condo facilities there is the distinct possibility of packs of roaming dogs on the loose. Nothing could be more upsetting to a non-dog lover than a situation in which dogs come romping through the common area at unexpected times of the day or night.

For example, a retired couple had this to say: "We have too many dogs for a town house development. They are let out in the dark to perform their destruction on shrubs and yards."

A sales manager, who later moved out, said, "Dogs tore up garbage, ruined lawns and shrubs, and were a common nuisance."

Dog control is a serious problem in a condominium environment and should be an important part of any condo's rules and regulations.

Split Conversions. Many high-rise condominiums, as has been noted in an earlier chapter, have been converted from rental apartments into condo units. The usual direction of conversion is from rental unit to condo unit. However, in some instances—particularly in a large condominium during a slow real estate season—certain condominium high-rise owners have taken to renting unsold apartments.

The mixture of rental apartments and condominium units is always a risky one. The condo unit owner feels that the rental units in the same building "bring down the value" of all the condo units. Real estate experts indeed believe that rented units *do* lower the long-term value of the condo units and consequently drive down sales prices on condo units up for sale.

"Owners who rent are not desirable," one respondent said, "since renters disregard homeowner regulations. Condominiums should not be sold for speculation, but for residences only."

"I don't like developers to encourage renters by selling town houses for investment purposes," another added.

Owners can sometimes be prevented from renting out unsold condo units; in other cases, they cannot be. Laws have been passed in certain localities forbidding "mixed" conversions. Check your area carefully.

Condominium Association. As has been said before, a condominium is only as good as the condo association that runs it.

One blue-collar worker didn't like much about his association at all. His comment: "I don't appreciate the restrictions of the association. It's just too socialistic for me."

The condo unit owner who is saddled with an amateurish, incompetent, or ineffective association can expect only trouble. Maintenance will not be kept up; security may be lax; there may be a freewheeling ignoring of all the house rules; or there may be chaos in management generally.

Poor Construction. One feature that was commented on freely by many of the condo owners interviewed was the poor construction of some of the condominiums.

Today most states have laws that spell out the kind of construction necessary for any condominium—ruling out anything below a certain standard. But it is a good idea to have an engineer go over the construction of the condo unit before you decide to buy it. The unit is going to be your home, and you are going to be paying for it. It should be up to a standard that will give you good living.

Dishonest Salespeople. Another cry frequently heard from condo unit owners has to do with the scruples of the salespeople who have shown the property and sold it to them.

Condominium salespeople are no sharper or more crooked than real estate salespeople who deal in homes or apartments. Most of the average condo owner's prejudice against salespeople dates back to the time before the sales of condos were regulated by the state. Nowadays, there may be sharp operators around, but they are usually limited by laws that have been passed to protect the buyer and are not able to pull as many "tricks" as they once did.

Nevertheless, it is a good idea to read up in advance on condos and to know just about as much as you can before you put yourself in the hands of any salesperson. Your own knowledge of the property to be bought will protect you from the temptation of the salesperson to overlook certain disadvantages and oversell certain advantages.

But Is It for You?

Analyzing what people who live in condominiums think about them can tell you about the good features and the bad features the people interviewed have encountered. Nevertheless, what *they* think about condos and feel about the life they lead in them is confined to their own experiences.

How condominium life might affect *you* is another story entirely. Don't forget, condominium life is a way of life that is different from any other—light-years away from the conventional single-house life of suburbia. It is a mixture of small-town life, Army base life, pioneer community life, communal-living life, country club life, island life—and bits and pieces of almost every other kind of life you can imagine.

Essentially, it is a cooperative lifestyle that depends on the close social relationships of the people who live within the condo facilities and share the mutual benefits. As such, it depends on strict obedience to the rules of the condominium homeowners association. Obedience to the rules means that although you may want to paint your town house a certain color, your association may not permit you to do so.

Condominium life depends on immediate payment of assessments voted by the homeowners association. It depends on a total and—it could be said—slavish subservience to the overall community esprit. It depends on a social way of life that just may not be your cup of tea.

PSYCHOLOGICAL PROFILE OF THE CONDO-PHILE

Psychologically, condo living is a way of life for an extrovert, a group-oriented, outward-reaching person, a commingler, a total social person. It is also a way of life for someone who chances to be alone but doesn't *want* to be alone—singles, divorcées, retirees.

It is *not* the way of life for an introvert, a person who does not like large groups of people around, who avoids noise, sociable gatherings, and group games. And it is not the life for someone who is beginning to come unraveled because of too close contact with other people and wants to get away by himself on his private hours to get it all together again.

In the preceding studies a large group of condo owners were questioned in order to find out what appealed and didn't appeal to them about condominium living.

But it's sometimes more revealing to analyze individuals separately and find the way each one looks at condo life in order to get a more in-depth picture of both the appealing and unappealing aspects of the lifestyle.

How Communal Is Condo Communal?

Gregariousness and solitariness are two different psychological aspects that sometimes are in direct conflict in the human psyche. It is the *degree* of gregariousness you are attuned to that must be understood before deciding to move into a condominium environment.

For example, here's the reaction of a married woman who moved into a busy suburban condominium after living in a house in a small suburban town. We'll call her Mrs. Smithers.

"There's no such thing as a backyard in our condominium," she told a friend. "When I went out in the yard in my house, everything there was all mine. Here the outside area belongs to everyone.

"In fact, the outside is controlled by the homeowners association, and you need permission to do *anything.* You have to conform. You can't paint your front door sky blue or pink—it has to stay as it is, which is black. If you put on a storm door, you have to conform to a standard model.

"Some people may object to the conformity," Mrs. Smithers added. "I don't. I've wanted this for a long time."

INSTANT FRIENDSHIP AND TOGETHERNESS

Another couple who like the communal life lived to the hilt are the Christophersons, a young couple with a four-year-old daughter.

"It's instant friendship," Mr. Christopherson explained. "We lived in an apartment in the city, where there were 1,600 families. You know, we didn't socialize with our neighbors at all.

"Here, we've already met six or seven couples who have become real friends! And I'm sure there are many more to come."

As for Mrs. Christopherson, she has some ideas herself about the kinds of lifestyles she might run into if she moved elsewhere.

"I'm sure I wouldn't find the same kind of camaraderie we have here in a house in a small town. I lived in one when I was growing up. People are cliqueish, and there's a 'separate' feeling. You're not *together* the way we are here. I wouldn't change it for anything."

Mr. Christopherson likes particularly the spontaneous parties that tend to start up without any determined effort.

"We meet people at the swimming pool and the tennis courts," he said, "and the development has two or three big parties a year. Each family brings a gourmet dish and for about four dollars a family you can stuff yourself until you can't eat anymore. It's a lot like an old-fashioned Manhattan block party."

"All You Hear at Night Is the Leaves Falling"

The Mortimers left an apartment in the city for a country town house located in a wooded area of the suburbs to get more space for their three children. They are people who like their privacy. Their low-density project is located in a country-like setting, with each unit owner having title to the land his condo stands on.

The project resembles a suburban neighborhood with private gardens and wooded countryside. The Mortimers still go into the city for their occasional fling at night life. But that's only to balance up the privacy they have found in their country town house in the wooded suburbs.

Mrs. Mortimer recalled: "In the city, we had a neighbor upstairs who practiced the piano twelve hours a day. It drove us crazy. Here all you hear at night is the leaves falling."

Needless to say, they love it.

The Allens live in a slightly larger version of the Mortimers' country-style condominium. Their development is denser, their group more gregarious.

There aren't many children, but those who do live there spend most of their time outside the small backyard gardens. Because the condo is located in a fairly wooded area, the kids roam the woods and streams, hunting for salamanders and worms. About a dozen youngsters have full possession of the swimming pool most all the time.

The Allens still keep an apartment in New York. Mr. Allen lives there during the week near his job; he works as an engineer at night at a television station.

"The apartment is just a box," he explained. "You don't know when you wake up whether it's winter or summer or day or night."

He loves the feeling of the countryside and the fresh air and the woods.

"I WOULDN'T GO OUTDOORS IF YOU PAID ME"

Not everyone loves the great outdoors. The Forsythes moved into a high-rise condominium after leaving a single house on a large acreage in an expensive suburb.

"It was the nicest feeling last winter," Mrs. Forsythe said, "sitting indoors during the snow storm, knowing that somebody else would be doing the shoveling."

Many condo owners are retirees who have decided to shed their homeowning burdens.

"I like the unit I live in very much," said Mr. Jameson, a bachelor who moved out to the suburbs from the city after retiring. "I figure if I'm happy inside the house, there's no reason for me to go outside. I can entertain myself, eat, and sleep inside. Who needs the outdoors to give you colds and viruses? I wouldn't go outdoors if you paid me!"

Mr. Jameson has a large picture window in the family room of his unit. The scene he sees outside is a beautifully wooded area with a quiet lake at the end of it.

"See? That's what I like about the outdoors. It *looks* clean. That's enough for me. I'll take my indoor life any day."

... 10

How the Management Structure Works

A SMOOTHLY run household is the result of combining a knowledge of effective household management with the application of good housekeeping habits. The same is true of a smoothly run condominium.

Yet in a condominium, the owner of the condo unit does not have any part in the actual management of the entire project—except in an indirect, advisory way. The running of the functioning condominium is usually in the hands of a professional condominium manager—a job classification akin to the manager of a well-run hotel or to the supervisor of a well-run apartment building.

In most large condominiums—those having over 100 units—a manager and a staff usually are hired to keep the project running efficiently. In smaller projects—fifteen or twenty units—the homeowners association may elect one of their own people to manage the condominium.

The key to the whole concept of condominium management lies in the homeowners association. In order to find out how this association comes into existence, let's start at the beginning of a condominium project and follow its development through until both management structure and function become clear.

STEP ONE: CASTLES IN THE AIR

The condominium, like any single-family home, begins in the imagination of the builder. The builder does not actually call himself a builder; usually he calls himself a developer or entrepreneur. It is he who "gets things done"; it is he who raises a certain amount of "seed" money in order to start the project in the first place.

Once the money is available, the developer first of all buys an appropriate piece of land and then hires an architect to draw up plans to his requirements. He then takes the finished plans to a bank or other lending institution and, on the strength of the plans, persuades its officials to allocate money to begin the project.

When the money is found, the developer then hires a contractor to buy materials and hire workers to start construction. At the same time, he hires real estate salesmen, has a "plat" built—a miniature representation of what the entire project will look like when it is finished—and begins an advertising campaign to sell living units in the projected condominium.

Let's suppose that the plat looks good, the location selected is a popular one, and people are found who want to buy condominium units in the projected complex. Of fifty places in the finished project, he immediately sells two units.

STEP TWO: THE BUILDING BEGINS TO GO UP

Up to this point, nothing has actually been built on the property. But with two units sold, the builder goes ahead and has his contractor begin work. The condominium starts to take shape and rise from the ground.

As each unit is sold, incidentally, the buyer is told what

percentage of the entire condominium's common interest he holds with his unit. The owner of a two-bedroom unit will own a higher percentage of the common interest than the owner of a one-bedroom unit; the owner of a three-bedroom unit will of course own an even higher percentage of the common interest. In fact, owners on higher floors will usually own larger percentages, as well those whose views are superior.

With the building still in the process of going up, there is no actual managing to be done, but the builder is "in charge" of everything on the property. The owners of projected units are usually not obligated to pay management fees for maintenance and upkeep on the common areas until they physically take possession of the units.

In our hypothetical case history, the builder has good luck and sells three more units. At some time during these months when the building is rising, he calls together his five unit owners and explains the mechanics of condominium operation so that they will know how it works when they move in.

STEP THREE: THE ASSOCIATION IS CONCEIVED

He appoints these five owners as members of an advisory committee on management, which will later become the nucleus of the condo's homeowners association, to which all owners will belong. In order to acquaint his small group with the intricacies of condominium management, he sends his cadre to observe the activities of a functioning association.

They visit the board of directors of a condominium homeowners association the builder himself began a year before. The committee attends several meetings of the homeowners association and begins to draw up plans for their own association, to be convened when the first owners begin moving in.

By studying the rules and regulations of other condominiums, the committee draws up a set of rules governing the recreational facilities, the common areas, and other matters.

Five other units are sold, and the committee of five begins welcoming new members, explaining the organizational setup to them. Soon twenty-five units are sold. By now new owners and newcomers are all on friendly terms with one another.

The great day arrives when the first units in the condominium are ready for occupancy. The first ten owners move in. Condominium management fees—upkeep and maintenance that will keep the project running—are now set by the builder. From experience, he knows exactly how much it will cost.

During the association's first months, he himself acts as manager, taking care of all cleaning up, repairs, services, and so on. Soon thirty-five units are sold. By now twenty-five of the families have moved in; half the condominium is occupied.

STEP FOUR: THE ASSOCIATION IS BORN

Now the owners and the builder meet and an association of homeowners is formed in accordance with the provisions in the enabling declaration. The advisory committee submits its rules and regulations for a vote by the entire association. The association accepts, and they are in business—a legally constituted body.

With the builder presiding, a group of owners is elected to form a board of directors to run the association: president, vice-president, secretary, treasurer, and director-at-large.

Because of his position, the builder is still a member of the board of directors, ex officio, with vote. Although the board operates the condominium, the builder himself still controls the board through a majority vote, since the total number of unsold units (each unit has one vote) is more than the five members of the board.

The builder continues to act as manager of the condominium, at this point hiring a professional manager with good credentials to do the daily hiring and firing of condominium staff members, along with the purchasing of supplies and the hiring of services to keep the project going.

Families continue to move in every day. A maintenance and upkeep fee is determined by taking an average of the amount of money needed to run the condo for several months. The total is divided proportionately among the unit owners according to the percentage of their ownership. The maintenance and upkeep fee is collected each month.

The final fifteen units are sold, and the buyers move in. The builder surrenders his position on the board of directors and leaves.

STEP FIVE: THE ASSOCIATION IS ON ITS OWN

The management of the condominium is now in the hands of the owners of the living units. The builder is out of the picture entirely. The hired manager now becomes an employee of the board of directors representing the association of owners, and is wholly responsible to it.

Of course, the management profile sketched here is an ideal one, in which the condominium is a success from the start, with the builder a man of experience, with the financial situation at the moment perfect, and with no obstacles or problems facing the association.

It is needless to say that such an ideal situation *could* occur, but it is highly unlikely that it *would.* There are always one or two problems that manage to crop up. We'll look at them later.

It is important to note that the maintenance fee is the crux of condominium management. Out of the maintenance fee comes the salary of the manager, once the builder has left. Out of the maintenance fee come the salaries of the staff and the money which pays for all services rendered to the condominium, including fixed costs and reserve costs. Since the maintenance fee provides the money that goes to operate the condominium, and is fundamental to the entire management picture, it is important to consider it in detail.

THE MAINTENANCE FEE

Operation and upkeep services paid for out of the maintenance fee vary significantly from one development to the next. The services, however, are usually broken down into five specific categories:

- Management costs
- Operational costs
- Maintenance costs
- Fixed costs
- Reserve costs

Costs of Condominium Management. Management costs generally include the following:

- Manager's salary
- Legal fees
- Accounting fees
- Social Security and withholding for staff
- Office expenses
- Other management costs

The manager's fee may be paid to the builder of the condominium, especially in the early months of the project. However, once all units are sold, the builder turns over the management to the homeowners association. The association, through its board of directors, then runs the condominium.

Most condominium associations find the onus of running the entire project too complex and frustrating for a nonprofessional. They hire a professional manager and staff to run maintenance and upkeep operations.

The condominium staff hired by the manager or provided by a management group can vary from one condominium to the other. A large condominium will have a doorman at the entrance to the building. Perhaps a full-time gardener will be employed. There may be any number of staff members, depending on the size of the project. All these salaries are paid out of the maintanence fee.

In addition to the manager's fee—he may actually be one of the unit owners who is an experienced professional —most condominiums need a lawyer on retainer in case legal problems arise. Cases could arise between unit owners, between the condominium itself and neighboring projects or corporations, or between the condominium and the city.

It is obvious that preparation of the maintenance budget is a complicated procedure. Many large condominiums have accountants on retainer throughout the year to advise in the preparation of all budgets and to go over the assets (or deficits) before and after each monthly payment.

The presence of an accountant also ensures each unit owner that his bills—the total amount he pays each month for upkeep and maintenance—are honestly and accurately rendered. Not only is this a most necessary precaution for determining monthly bills, but also for determining certain maintenance fees on an owner's income tax if he is questioned by the Internal Revenue Service.

The salaries paid to all staff members—be it a small staff or a large one—must conform to federal regulations. Social Security taxes must be paid to the government, and income tax payments withheld from staff salaries and paid to the Internal Revenue Service.

Typical expenses in the management office should not be large, but can sometimes escalate greatly, especially if the association board wants notices mailed out or other jobs undertaken by the secretarial staff. Expenses also include costs of stationery, postage, and telephone.

Some leeway must be allowed for "other management costs," just in case something comes up which is not covered in legal, accounting, and management fees.

Costs of Operating the Condominium. Operational costs usually include the following:

- Utilities (water, electricity, gas)
- Heat for the clubhouse and swimming pool
- Water for landscape gardening

Utility bills for electric power, water, and heat for the clubhouse and swimming pool, landscape, foyer, and halls include those for the common property of the condominium but do not include each owner's unit, of course. Each owner will pay his utility bills on his own; cost of water and electric bills are based on meters in each unit.

Depending on the condominium's design, the overall heating—particularly if it emanates from a central heating system—will be allocated to the common property utility bills. Otherwise, if heat comes from each condo unit's separately metered heat—such as electric power for heating and air conditioning—it will be billed to each separate unit owner.

In some communities utility costs will be much higher

than in others. It is a good idea to find out what typical operating costs will come to for a month. Heating and air-conditioning will vary—heating higher in the winter, air-conditioning higher in the summer—but the electricity and water costs will probably run about the same throughout the year.

Costs of Condominium Maintenance. Maintenance costs usually include the following:

- Janitorial services
- Trash and garbage disposal
- Window washing
- Grounds maintenance and equipment
- Heavy equipment maintenance
- Craft equipment repairs
- Building maintenance
- Snow removal
- Swimming pool maintenance
- Security

Most condominium unit owners must pay for garbage removal. This fee includes not only the money paid out to the garbage collectors but that paid for any incidental haulaways that may be required by weather conditions, strikes, or other emergencies.

Grounds maintenance includes not only lawns, shrubs, and trees, but upkeep of sidewalks, streets, alleys, and pathways. Potholes in driveways and streets owned as common property by the condominium must be filled in. Sidewalks and pathways must be kept in good repair in order to prevent lawsuits from condo unit owners or outsiders, who might fall and hurt themselves.

Maintenance, repair, and occasional replacement of equipment—power mowers, pool filtering equipment, clubhouse air conditioner or furnace, tools, poolside furniture, clubhouse equipment, and so on—must be covered and considered as an ongoing expense.

Equipment of all kinds wears out with usage, sometimes much faster than most people realize. There are also frequent repairs necessary for all mechanical equipment used in maintaining property. Gasoline, oil, and other fuel necessary to run power equipment must also be considered in this section of the budget.

Heavy equipment maintenance and repairs must also be included. In large condominiums there are sometimes trucks, buses, fire engines, golf carts, and delivery trucks used in the day-to-day operation of the project. Keeping these in good repair and fueling them takes a great deal of money that must be allocated ahead of time.

Maintenance of sports facilities such as billiard tables, bowling pins and alleys, and tennis courts is another consideration. In large condominiums with extensive recreational areas—in particular for hobbies and crafts—special equipment such as power tools necessary for the hobbies must be kept in good shape.

If there are other recreational services in addition to a swimming pool, they will have to be included in the total cost for maintenance. Some maintenance costs come only at various seasons of the year—snow removal, for one— but must be included in the general average to give you a fair estimate of the amount of money you will be spending for overall maintenance throughout the year and to avoid sudden unexpected charges.

Maintenance fees vary widely. The more elaborate the facilities, the higher the budget allocation. Nicely manicured lawns and beautiful flower beds need extra care. If a swimming pool needs a full-time lifeguard, that means a full-time salary, with Social Security and income tax withholding. Operating expenses include elevator maintenance, heating maintenance, and air-conditioning maintenance. A golf course means a heavy outlay of money not only for the layout of the course but for greens upkeep as well.

Fixed Costs of Condominium Management. Fixed costs usually include the following:

- Insurance
- Elevator maintenance
- Building upkeep (paint, weather stripping, etc.)
- Gardening
- Special assessments

Insurance premiums for liability, property damage, workmen's compensation, bonds for those handling association funds, and so on are all part of the maintenance fees. Funds to pay for these premiums and bonds, for possible property damage, and for other fees needed by any condominium must be provided.

All these expenses are included in the typical condominium maintenance and upkeep budget. The coverage must be adjusted from time to time, depending on the going rates. Also, if any of the policies become collectible, the premiums will escalate.

Money must be allocated to pay for replacement of nursery stock or new landscaping. Weather can cause great havoc with trees, shrubs, flower beds, and grass. In extremely hot weather, grass can turn brown and be burned so badly it must be completely replaced. In extremely cold weather, trees, shrubs, and foundation plants can be lost.

Soil can erode and leave large areas denuded of growth during especially severe winter storms. Replacement of soil and leveling and smoothing off of landscape contours can put a severe strain on the grounds budget. Not only that, in many cases extra gardeners must be hired to keep newly planted stock healthy until it matures fully.

Communities levy special assessments such as sewer assessments or flood control assessments in various ways, some including these fees in the real estate tax and others billing them separately. You are liable to all these levies by the city or county and should be prepared for them.

Reserve Costs of Condominium Management. Reserve costs usually include the following:

• Emergency repair to common facilities
• Emergency replacement of common carpets, furniture, etc.
• Emergency alterations to common facilities
• Other reserve funds

Funds for the establishment of a cash reserve usually amount to 3 to 5 percent of the total gross budget of the condominium. Emergencies are bound to arise—if not in one particular area, in another. Because crises must be met quickly, there must be cash on hand to pay for services that have not been anticipated. In some condominiums, even more than 5 percent of the gross budget is allocated to such emergencies.

The unit owner himself must pay for emergency repair to his own premises. But when something happens to a part of the project that is held in common among all owners—for example, an outside wall damaged by a falling tree in a gale—the cost of the repair must be borne by everyone through the means of a reserve fund set aside especially for such emergencies.

The same is true of simple repair problems like the wearing out of common carpeting or the depreciating of furniture or property belonging to the common areas of the project.

The homeowners association may vote at any time to alter or repair the common facilities. To prevent the need for a special assessment for such an alteration or improvement a special fund should be held in reserve at all times to provide for such an eventuality. The same is true of other unexpected drains on the common pocketbook. Reserve money should be set aside for them too.

RESPONSIBILITY OF MANAGEMENT

The responsibility assumed by the manager of a condominium is wide-ranging and complex. There is a need for such a manager to know a great deal about budgets, collection services, maintenance and cleaning services, security services, and even the psychological means of keeping unit owners satisfied and happy.

Each service provided must be well defined by the management. It must also be budgeted in a clear and unequivocal fashion. Each owner must be able to see *exactly* how much he is paying for each specific service the management is providing for him. He should be able to anticipate how much he will have to pay for the oncoming year rather than be subjected to sudden unexplained and unprecedented rises in the monthly maintenance fee.

The manager must be able to project the budget accurately, basing it on previous figures. In the case of a beginning project which has no previous costs the fledgling manager might call in a professional consultant to work out such a projection.

Beware of any condominium which does not have a manager who can give you maintenance fee projections. If the manager happens to be the builder, it is a good idea to question him closely on the maintenance and operating budget. His maintenance fee projections may be deliberately underestimated in order to help him sell units. It is necessary to find out *exactly* what is included in the maintenance fee and the costs which are projected.

WHEN SALES BEGIN TO SLUMP. . . .

From a study of the number of steps it is necessary to take to effect smooth-running condominium management, you can begin to see how certain abuses by the builder/developer can begin to creep into the condo picture. Not all condominiums go up and become filled with the ease of the hypothetical one you have studied.

The first hitch that develops usually occurs during the first months of the condo's sales campaign, when the builder is trying to sell living units to prospective customers. One of several things may happen to put a damper on sales:

1. The location may be bad. The builder may have been unable to buy the piece of property he really wanted and has been forced to settle for second or third best. On the other hand, he may have selected a bad piece of property from simple ignorance.

2. The housing market may suddenly reverse itself and become a buyer's market. That means that there are hundreds of competing units on the market. People do not want to buy a piece of pie in the sky; most of them want to purchase something that is already built, something that is already functioning smoothly.

3. Delays—man-made or God-made—may intervene and slow up construction. Upset because they have no place to live, many buyers may back out, leaving units unsold. Delays never help anyone; strikes, floods, supply shortages are no one's friends.

. . . THE BUILDER MAY PANIC

There are dozens of reasons why condo unit sales may flag. But when they do, it becomes a desperate matter for the builder to try to fill the building. It is at this point that he may begin to panic and put into effect actions that may be fraught with problems for unit owners.

For example, a builder with a half-dozen empty units in a finished condo may suddenly decide to get rid of all his sales force, cut out the ads, and rent the units until the market picks up again.

This in effect is conversion in the reverse direction. It is an unsatisfactory situation for the condo unit owners; rented property is never as exclusive as sold property. In fact, a psychological change takes place in the image of the condo. It loses stature. The condominium units lose market value—sometimes to an astonishing degree.

The owner of a unit feels cheated. Because he feels his investment is being hurt by the presence of rented units near him, he may begin looking around for a buyer. The builder has changed the condos to rentals in the first place because there were no buyers. Everyone is angry with the situation.

Many condominium by-laws include provisions to prevent the owner/developer from renting out units that are for sale. Some do not. If there are no such provisions, you should understand that you are taking a risk by buying without legal protection against such rentals.

There are other ways the builder can try to dig himself out of a bad financial hole. The key factor in several of these real estate ploys, once again, is lodged in the management structure. Let's look at one example.

One builder set up a professional management organization with other people to front for him and hired them on during his early months as overseer of the fledgling homeowners association. At first the organization performed its management services effectively and efficiently.

At a point just before the builder finally turned the association over to the owners, he signed a noncancellable contract with his own management group. With the management in his hands, he was able to cut back on quality and continue charging the same amount he had before. The case went to the courts.

The importance of the management structure cannot be overstressed. You must examine carefully the function and efficiency of your condominium manager. As a member of the homeowners association you are responsible for hiring him. If you don't like what he is doing, remove him and replace him with a competent manager.

The manager manages, but the association—through its board of directors—*really* runs the condominium from the wings. Ultimately, you run the condo.

Now let's take a look at the homeowners association and how it works.

...11

Minigovernment:
The Homeowners Association

THE homeowners association is the heart and soul of the condominium. The association hires the manager through its board of directors; the association pays the bills through its fees and assessments; the association polices its members, making the rules and regulations by which the condominium is run; the association deals with wrongdoers and transgressors.

While the association is a nonpolitical body, it is nevertheless a type of minigovernment, with local power to run things, change things, lay down laws, and even collect assessments. And it is a proprietary organization. It not only runs things, but it owns what it runs.

WHAT MEMBERSHIP MEANS TO YOU

When you buy a living unit in a condominium, you automatically assume membership in the condominium homeowners association. It is your protection against tyrannical management over which you might have no control without the association. Because the association will manage and operate the common property you own with everyone else, it can affect your enjoyment of your own private property, the satisfaction you gain from your surroundings, how much you have to pay each month, and how valuable your investment turns out to be.

The point is, if you buy into any condominium, you had better pay close and strict attention to the perils and privileges that go with your compulsory membership in its association.

With an estimated 2,000,000 condominium unit owners in the country today, there are probably 20,000 homeowners associations in condominiums—assuming the average condo complex to be about 100 units. Yet despite this large number of associations and people belonging to them, not many really have any experience in setting up an association and making it work. And very few people who buy into them have any clear idea of what they are taking on.

Yet things must be done properly from the start, or there will be big trouble for you soon enough. The reason why is stated in the Urban Land Institute's publication, *Managing a Successful Community Association.*

> If a new business makes unwise policy decisions it simply ceases operation and goes out of existence. A community association does not have that option, for it will exist as long as the homes it serves continue to exist. If a community association is mismanaged, the homeowners will literally pay for those mistakes until they are rectified.

It is the builder who creates this minigovernment, and his interests are not necessarily the same as yours. His investment remains a risk until he eventually sells out. It is understandable that he arranges to hang on to the management controls and relinquishes them only gradually over a number of years.

Frankly, most builders don't know anything about running a community. Many of them hire a professional management firm to launch a condominium project. When you buy into the project, you look on the manager as a kind of "extension" of the builder.

If the management of the condo is good, you usually identify with and cooperate with the manager. But if a troubled builder has locked you into a high-priced, long-term contract with a bad manager, fireworks are sure to ensue.

Good leadership is your responsibility—the duty of each homeowner, of each member of the association.

ONE VOTE—ONE MAN

In almost all condominium homeowners associations you are entitled to one vote in any association matter if you are a unit owner. In some condominiums each owner may have a fraction of a vote or the vote may be weighted in one manner or other, to reflect the size of each unit. However, the general rule is to allot one vote to each unit owner. In condominium matters this rule of thumb carries out the Supreme Court's dictum: one vote, one man.

This allocation should not be confused with the percentage of maintenance fees you must pay as a unit owner, which is alloted to you in relation to the amount of area your unit covers, its location, and its view. This percentage, of course, refers to the percentage of the total expense budget that you pay in your monthly fees.

With your obvious responsibility spelled out for you by your ability to vote on issues regarding the maintenance, upkeep, governing, and operating of the condominium, you have only one duty: to attend meetings and to vote.

In fact, meetings are so important that provisions are always made to allow you to delegate your vote to your co-owner, if you have one, to a friend who can act as a proxy, or to a member of the board of directors who can act in your behalf to vote.

Nor is it enough to attend meetings simply to look on and vote. You must take part vigorously in discussions about the running and management of the condo. If you sit silent, you are doing yourself a disservice as well as everyone else. Meetings are held to receive input by unit owners; if you keep quiet, the current of input to the directors is restricted and the feeling of the majority may never really be known.

A MEETING OF THE ASSOCIATION

Meetings of the homeowners association are held on a regularly scheduled basis, usually quarterly (four times a year), semiannually, or annually. At least ten days to two weeks before each meeting, a notice will be exhibited on a bulletin board in a prominent place enjoining all members to participate.

Provisions for emergency meetings for the entire association are usually made in the bylaws, with the specified time for the posting of the notice prior to the meeting, the specified place, and any other additional facts that must be included.

Even though only one owner from each unit is entitled to vote, all who live in the unit are invited to attend the meeting. You as the owner are the only one able to vote, make motions, and second motions. But co-owners or co-habitants with you are entitled to take part in any discussion, participate in any activities, and express opinions about anything germaine to the meeting.

In order to differentiate between you as a voter and others attending the meeting, a special badge or other distinguishing emblem is affixed prominently, where the chairperson can clearly see it. Guests and co-owners can sit anywhere they wish, usually with their friends or spouses.

Before the meeting, the agenda will be sent around to each member along with the minutes of the previous general meeting—either by mail or by hand from the secretary of the board of directors. The agenda will include all the subjects to be discussed and/or voted on.

You always have a chance to bring up new business at the meeting, but if you do have anything you want to air in front of the assembled unit owners, you should contact the president of the board ahead of time, discuss it with him, and request that he put the subject on the agenda for proper action.

THE WORK OF THE COMMITTEES

As in most democratic political groups, the bulk of the work is performed by committees. Committees are composed of individual owners who have some related interest in the various areas of activity supervised by the committee.

For example, the grounds committee might be composed of owners who have a particular talent in gardening, landscaping, or horticulture generally. The grounds committee may be a standing or permanent committee in liaison continually with the grounds staff, if there is one, or the grounds consultant.

The swimming pool committee might be composed of one of the owners interested in running the swimming pool in an orderly fashion and perhaps another owner who understands first aid. A disciplinarian—someone who knows how to set up and enforce rules and regulations that are stringent enough and at the same time not too tough—might be a welcome addition to the pool committee.

The tennis committee might be composed of athletically inclined owners who like to play tennis and who understand the importance of the rules and regulations that govern the use of the court. In addition, there should be someone on the committee who knows how to assure court users that they all have equal access to the court.

The budget committee is a crucial one, for it is this group that actually oversees the entire money allocation toward the management of the condominium. It is the committee which eventually writes up the budget and makes sure the proper allocations of funds have been made. In turn, it is to this committee that complaints and suggestions can be made by members.

THE BOARD OF DIRECTORS

The actual governing body of the homeowners association—and hence, the *real* governing body of the condominium itself—is the board of directors.

As in most democratic political groups, the board of directors is simply a small select group of members of the association chosen by the total membership to make decisions for the association on a day-to-day basis. In short, the board of directors is a representative group of the association that carries on the work of the association between regular meetings.

Like most boards, the typical homeowners association board of directors contains an uneven number of directors—three, five, seven—so that action cannot bog down with a tie vote. And, like most boards of directors, the association board of directors also has in its nucleus the officers of the association.

Each member of the board of directors is elected for a

term of one year, two years, or three years—depending on the bylaws of the association. It is a good idea, incidentally, for the bylaws to specify office tenure in an overlapping fashion: for example, three years apiece for each director, with one or two dropping out each year. This allows for change as well as for continuity.

A MEETING OF THE BOARD

Board meetings should take place on a monthly basis. Enough happens in the average condominium for a number of problems to crop up week by week. By meeting every month, the board of directors is keeping on top of whatever problems have come up.

Just before each board meeting, the agenda and the minutes of the last meeting are sent out to each member of the board, with the time and date of the meeting clearly stated. When the board meets, minutes are discussed and passed, subjects on the agenda are discussed and action is taken on them—all by the rules of parliamentary procedure—and then the reports of the standing committees and any ad hoc committees that are operating are read and discussed.

The board either takes action or defers action to the regular association meeting, if a popular vote has to be taken. Most actions that come up before the board are specific ones and simply need a vote one way or the other.

DIRECTOR—A SERIOUS RESPONSIBILITY

Each director undertakes a great deal of responsibility to his neighbors when he assumes a role on the board. He is the person who in most cases deals directly with the members of the association if any kind of liaison is necessary. He must not only be compatible with the members of the association, but he must have enough clout to be able to deal with them responsibly.

A martinet will raise the hackles of every association member he deals with. A namby-pamby will nod and be a yes-man to everyone he sees. In either case, there will be bad rapport between board and association members.

An ideal director should be someone who is gregarious but not too susceptible with cliques. He should be level-headed but at the same time should be able to plunge into the breach if the occasion should warrant it.

He should be able to listen closely to what his constituents—the association members—are talking about. And he should be able to tell them when they are making excessive demands on the board of directors. He should be able to judge priorities—know the difference between a big problem and an infinitesimal gripe.

He should have a sense of balance, too. If he has a particular bias in favor of one course of action that is under contemplation, he should be able to bury his bias and act for the good of the majority. And he should be able to go all-out for what he believes in if he feels it is for the good of the association.

The perfect director doesn't exist—but there are those who approximate a model. If you are lucky, you will elect him to office. Perhaps you may be the one yourself.

OFFICERS OF THE ASSOCIATION

As soon as the association has elected its board of directors, the directors meet and elect officers. There are usually four officers in a typical board of directors for an association of up to 100 homeowners. They are: president, vice-president, secretary, and treasurer. On the boards of small condominiums—anywhere from twenty-five to fifty units—the offices of secretary and treasurer are usually combined.

In addition to the three or four officers above, the bylaws may call for one, two, or three directors-at-large.

The average size of a board of directors is around five people. For condominiums with 100 to 200 families, the size may vary from seven to eleven—even more in some instances. It is not wise to have too bulky a board of directors. It tends to resemble a town meeting, and takes more time or work to get things done.

"Take Me to Your Leader"

The office of *president* is the hub around which everything revolves in the government of the condominium. The president is the chairman of the board. He runs the board meetings. He runs the association meetings. He is the liaison man between the hired manager and the association of homeowners.

The president of the association is the person who must be all things to all people. He must be accessible, available, and must listen well. He must have excellent emotional balance, be able to hold his temper when all around him are losing theirs.

He must be a psychologist, a sociologist, and a philosopher. It is essential that he like people to begin with, for it is quite possible that before his tenure is up he will discover that he really doesn't like people quite so much as he thought he did.

Although only one part of his job entails presiding over meetings—board meetings, association meetings, committee meetings, special group meetings, and so on—it is essential that he know the rules for parliamentary procedure inside out.

He should have *Robert's Rules of Order* committed to memory before he sits down to chair his first meeting—otherwise the entire proceeding can well disintegrate into a shambles.

It is not easy for anyone to be fair to everybody, but it is essential in the person who presides over the myriad personnel that comprise a typical condominium association.

The president's authority is built into the job. In fact, he must make use of his authority or he is actually malingering in his duty. Authority spreads out from him in four different directions, and the individuals to whom it spreads become his helpers, or, if you like to think of it in a different way, his unpaid employees.

He uses his authority to provide action through four different means, each of which is delegated to him through the bylaws of the association—the manager, officers, directors, and committees. Of course, these are the same powers that the president or chairman of the board has in any democratic group.

MANAGER

The president's most important ally is the manager of the condominium. In a large condominium—say, 100 families—the association usually decides to hire a manager and management staff to do the tedious and specialized work necessary to run the condominium.

Even though the president's position is an unpaid one, he does represent the total power of all the owners of living units in the condo. That power is an awesome one: he literally holds the livelihood of the manager in the palm of his hand. An intelligent and efficient manager will cooperate with the president of the association. An intelligent and effective president will work in total cooperation with the manager, as the unpaid overseer that he is.

It is not the president's job to *run* the condominium, but to *see* that the condominium manager does a good job. He is there to inspire and to suggest rather than to terrorize or coerce. A good working relationship between president and manager is necessary for harmonious condominium management.

...12

The Condominium *Is* the Future

SEVERAL unrelated sociological, economic, and political trends of the past few years have coincided unexpectedly to make the condominium an exceptionally important symbol of the future and a new mode of housing for the American people.

These trends include the following:

• The breakdown of the conventional family unit and the corresponding rapid increase of singles, unmarrieds, and divorcés as unconventional family units

• The increase in the number of retirees—couples and singles—in the population at large

• The dramatic increase in the cost of the single-family house, coupled with the concurrent decrease in housing starts

• The tarnishing of the American dream of a house in the country and a car in every garage

• The international energy crisis and its ultimate effects on the design and placement of American communities

• The groping toward older values, particularly in the experimental communes of the 1960s

Let's see how these trends have combined almost inadvertently to make condominium living the attractive and viable thing it is today.

THE SINGLES EXPLOSION

The population figures for singles are an impressive reminder of how the phenomenon of the one-person family unit has grown in the past decade.

In 1970, for example, there were 43,900,000 "singles" in the twenty-to-thirty-four age group.

In 1978, there were 52,700,000 "singles"—a rise of just over 20 percent.

In fact, the "singles" rise started even before 1970. In the decade between 1960 and 1970, when the population as a whole was increasing by 16 percent, the population of singles was increasing by more than twice as much—by 39 percent. At the same time, the number of divorced and widowed was rising by 34 percent, evidence of the breakdown of the family as a living unit. Even more significant was the fact that in 1970 almost half of the singles —unmarried by their own choice or as a result of divorce —were under thirty-five years of age.

By 1978, more than one in ten households was headed by someone who had never been married! In the twenty-to-thirty-four age group, a growing number of men and women were either postponing marriage or passing it up entirely. It is this age group in which the number of singles is still increasing spectacularly.

The point is, a "singles" must live somewhere. It is difficult—if not impossible—for most singles to buy a traditional one-family house. It is far too expensive. And it is also difficult for them to rent apartments; these seem to be in scarcer and scarcer supply as housing starts dwindle.

The condominium is the obvious answer to the housing problem for those people who form the bulk of the new singles in America. This group is a most heterogeneous one. Some are unmarried men and women, some are divorced men and women, some are widows and widowers. They may live outside the pattern of conventional life, yet they must all live somewhere.

Some live alone; others live together, trying out new living "arrangements" instead of marriage. Others experiment with communal living of various kinds.

Single parents are a new phenomenon of our rapidly changing culture. Many are women who want to find themselves as individuals even if they do have children. Some are divorced, some are widowed, some are unmarried. Many are separated or divorced fathers with children to bring up and educate.

THE KINDS OF SINGLES TODAY

There are roughly five different kinds of singles: the willfully unmarrieds; divorcés; parenting singles of both sexes; widows and widowers; and retirees, both male and female.

All of them, as can be seen, are excellent prospects for the newly opened condominium lifestyle.

Most willfully unmarrieds—those who have never been married and don't intend to—now fall into the twenty-to-thirty-four age category. In the future there will be even more of them.

Divorcés cross all age groups, but by far the most today seem to be in the thirty-to-fifty category. Many of these seek out other partners, but many do not; obviously, for every divorce or separation, *two* housing units become necessary rather than just one.

Most parenting singles include people from twenty-five to forty years of age. Singles in this group are usually unable to pay the high price of a single-family house. The congenial, peculiarly communal life of the condominium is perfect for them.

Widows and widowers are generally older, although not necessarily so. Usually these singles don't have children to worry about because they have grown up to form their own family units. Widows and widowers are excellent prospects for the condominium lifestyle.

The fifth and last group of singles is composed of retirees, both male and female. The singles retirée is an excellent prospect for the condominium scene.

THE RETIRED COUPLES EXPLOSION

The phenomenon of early retirement coupled with the phenomenon of the increased life span for both male and female have combined to cause an unprecedented explosion in the number of retired people.

The condominium boom began in Florida, where couples bought into condominiums to live out their days in retirement. It has continued, not only there, but in other parts of the country as well.

The condominium lifestyle is most compatible with retirement. Now, thanks to its growth in other parts of the country and in many different guises, the condo is not confined to the high-rise-and-pool type first encountered, but appears in many different and varied guises, as we have seen.

THE HIGH COST OF SINGLE-FAMILY HOUSING

Inflation can be blamed for the escalating cost of homes that has put them out of the reach of most young marrieds. Indeed, it has almost put a home out of the reach of the average middle-class family.

Because the condominium is priced lower—30 percent

on the average—it becomes the most promising, viable alternative to the single-family home.

The condo can also act as a substitute for yesterday's "first home," the low-cost house that couples bought to live in for a while, before moving to a costlier home with more amenities.

THE ENERGY CRISIS

When the OPEC nations raised oil prices and precipitated the worldwide energy crisis several years ago, it became obvious that the normal lifestyle of millions of Americans would never be the same again. With gasoline headed for well over a dollar a gallon today, and heating oil going up to join it, the warning signals are out to be ignored only at your peril.

Suburban communities simply cannot afford to spread out much further. It costs too dearly to drive in from remote areas to work even now. Besides that, good undeveloped areas are becoming harder and harder to find. Suburban sprawl is in crisis. What better way to obviate the crisis than to move people closer to where they work and to house them together—in condominiums rather than small spread-out single-family units.

Urban and suburban planners realize that the suburbs are in trouble. Their outlook embraces more communal forms of living—such as the condominium in its many shapes and manifestations.

With public transportation making a massive comeback in some areas and foreseen in others, you would be able to get from your condominium directly to work without the use of a private car. And with the energy crisis persisting, you might not be able to afford to maintain that car in the not-too-distant future.

THE COMMUNES OF TOMORROW

During the turbulent 1960s, many Americans sought a new lifestyle in communal living. In fact, the commune of the sixties was not far removed from the early Colonial town of New England. Nor was it very far removed from the Greek city-state.

This search for new values was inspired in part by the feeling of alienation that overtook young people during the postwar years—the 1950s and 1960s. The country—only 100,000,000 in population at the beginning of the century—had boomed fantastically to 200,000,000 during that era.

The individual felt overwhelmed by the numbers of people around him. Every facet of life was crowded, and the crowding caused many more sensitive persons to become lost in the wilderness of people.

Communal living—no matter what kind—brings people together, with common problems and common enjoyments shared. It exchanges the impersonal lifestyle of the big city for a more personal, friendly, relaxed mode of living.

One sociologist explained it in this fashion: "The wish to restore a sense of community, which some families feel has been lost in neighborhoods of widely spaced, detached homes, is being realized in the boom in condominium living."

Young people are primarily involved, according to a real estate broker. "There is an advantage to the younger, first-time buying couple, which is taken into account by the bank when they apply for a mortgage to a condominium. The condo lets these fledgling buyers afford a living unit for which they might not otherwise qualify financially."

GETTING TOGETHER AND SOLVING PROBLEMS

Today's condominium is a commune in essence. Psychologically, it is an answer to the alienation and disillusion of the recent past. Communal living exemplifies the idea of people getting together and solving their problems through cooperation.

For example, a group of renters threatened with eviction found that the way to beat the landlord at the game of conversion is to get together with their neighbors and do it themselves before it can be done to them. It is a difficult, back-breaking effort, but once you are successful, you feel that you have actually had a hand in controlling your own destiny.

The main consideration is that you eliminate the profit of the middleman—the dealer who buys the building at a relatively low figure, makes cosmetic rather than crucial improvements, and then sells individual condo units at a substantial profit. By bypassing the middleman, you can plow a great deal more money into the purchase price and the rehabilitation of the building and still buy your unit for less than the current market price.

Once you have gone through a conversion effort with your neighbors, your immediate acquaintances are definitely a more cohesive, tightly knit, and close community group than you were as renters.

THE DO-IT YOURSELF CONVERSION

This is a fairly new development, but it seems to be gaining steadily in popularity. It started back in the early 1970s, the story goes, when a longtime renter in an apartment building in a large city was scanning the real estate section of his newspaper.

When he spotted an ad for the sale of the building in which he lived, he immediately sensed traumatic days ahead and rightly guessed that the buyer would probably convert the apartment to condominium apartment units and sell his out from under him.

He gave a party, invited all his neighbors in, and told them that the building was up for sale. He then outlined a plan for raising enough money to buy the building among themselves and convert it to condominium status, then purchase the units for themselves. It was not quite a matter of "no sooner said than done," but the raising of the money, the purchase of the building, and the eventual conversion were successful.

Other apartment renters faced with possible eviction because of eventual conversion took notice of the amount of money the do-it-yourselfers had saved by converting their own property and started to form groups for the same purpose.

Soon a modus operandi had been established, one which is still used and can serve to forestall outside conversion of apartment units.

THE WAY TO DO THE JOB

It goes like this:
• Renters threatened with possible eviction meet to decide whether or not everyone in the building is interested in conversion.

• Next step is to determine if everyone is ready to purchase his own unit.

• After that, a promise is made to work together until the conversion is effected.

• Eventually an adviser, who has been through a conversion, is approached to act as a consultant on financial steps to be taken.

- A nonprofit corporation is founded by the tenants.
- The corporation elects a president, who approaches the owner of the building and makes him an offer.
- The adviser provides guidance and organizational know-how in leading the group through the labyrinthine sales negotiations.
- If things go well, the owner agrees to sell the building to the corporation.
- The building changes hands.
- The corporation makes an enabling declaration, changing the building into a condominium regime.
- Acting as owner, the corporation in turn sells each condominium unit to each separate buyer.
- The buyers form an association, take over the condominium from the corporation, and elect officers to run the condo.

"It's not so complex overall," one man who has been through it says, "but little things keep cropping up. The most important element is to move fast once you get the idea. If you delay, you may lose your building to the middleman—and that will cost you money."

Every conversion in which tenants have bought their building, he warns, has been fraught with rumor, intrigue, and panic. Tenants spearheading any conversion effort are looked upon with suspicion, disbelief, fear, and loathing by others.

"You need someone who knows how to play the game," he advises. "First of all, know enough to *know* that you *don't* know how to play."

THE DUPLEX CONDO CONVERSION

Currently there is a new wrinkle to the do-it-yourself conversion condominium. It's called the do-it-yourself duplex conversion condo. There are many good reasons why the double conversion works so well.

- It's a hedge against inflation.
- It's a solution to the problem of the overpriced single-family house.
- It's a good way to solve the problem of the younger, first-home buyer without enough big money to afford a home.
- It's in line with the sharp decrease in the number of persons per household in recent years.
- And it's part of a spreading interest in older houses for their aesthetic values.

For example, a bachelor in his twenties who decided he wanted to own his own house purchased a large old duplex in a suburb near a large city. But he had no intention of living in it all by himself.

Instead, he converted the house immediately into a two-unit condominium. The conversion cost about $1,000 in paperwork. Then, after moving into one of the units, he put the second unit on the market and sold it to a childless couple who both worked in the city.

He had bought the house for $90,000. He sold the condominium unit for $60,000. He actually bought his own condo unit for $31,000, including the $1,000 in paperwork—with an instant resale value of $60,000 and a profit of $29,000! Not bad for a man who was used to renting an apartment in the city.

There are lots of older houses which can easily be broken up into separate living units.

"I had to do something about spiraling costs," says another singles commuter, who bought a duplex in a suburban community forty-five miles from a large city and converted it to a condo. "I read the trends. I know I will be able to sell more easily when the time comes."

A professional couple, anxious to take a chance on a

communal lifestyle in which they both believed, bought a large three-story older house for $79,500. They split it up into three separate units, converted to a condominium, and sold the units immediately: one to a single woman parenting two children and the other to a retired couple who couldn't face living with a lot of other *old* people, isolated from the young.

"You know," the wife of the converter couple says, "this multifamily house is beginning to provide a kind of life-style that is very attractive to the two of us. Compared to the car-in-every-garage mystique we went through in the 1950s, it's a kind of beautiful life—something that we like to think of as the way of the future. It's—it's definitely chic."

Bibliography

PERIODICALS

Arneson, Howard D. "Business Outlook." *Business Week*, March 5, 1979.

Bayliss, John. "Condominium." *Holiday*, July 1973.

"Behind the Comeback of Condominiums." *U.S. News & World Report*, November 13, 1978.

"Big Switch to Condos and Co-ops." *Time*, March 5, 1979.

Birnbaum, Stephen. "Getting Away." *Esquire*, September 1977.

Bloom, Murray Teigh. "Is a Condominium Right for You?" *Readers Digest*, April 1974.

Burlingame, Carl. "Directory of Timeshare Resorts." *Holiday*, September 1977.

"Condominiums—Why All the Complaints." *U.S. News & World Report*, June 24, 1974.

DeHaan, Jon. "Key to Your Condo." *Holiday*, September/October 1976.

Ellis, Karen, and Taddeo, Frank. "Condominiums: What They Are, What They Aren't." *Retirement Living*, February 1976.

"Facts to Know About Condominiums." *Changing Times*, October 1973.

"Five Myths About Condominiums." *Changing Times*, December 1976.

Heineman, Nancy. "Calling a Condominium Home." *Essence*, May 1978.

"Housing: The Condo Caper." *Newsweek*, March 25, 1974.

"Housing: The Condo Craze." *Newsweek*, August 20, 1973.

Hunt, Avery. "Alternative Lifestyles: Cooperatives and Condominiums." *American Home*, May 1976.

Ingersoll, John H. "Inflation Hedge: A Financing Plan for Buying Condominiums." *House Beautiful,* June 1975.

Nader, Ralph. "Ralph Nader Reports: Condominium Pitfalls." *Ladies Home Journal,* August 1974.

"The New Homeowner Associations: They Run Things, Own Things, and You Have to Join." *Changing Times,* September 1974.

Nixon, Susan. "Do-It-Yourself Condomania." *Chicago,* March 1978.

"The Papers That Make You a Condominium Owner." *Changing Times,* June 1975.

Schoenstein, Ralph. "A Piece of the Rock or a Slice of the Clock." *Saturday Evening Post,* September 1976.

"Straight Talk from Owners on Condominium Living." *American Home,* September 1973.

"Suppose Your Apartment 'Goes Condominium.'" *Changing Times,* October 1974.

Tamarkin, Bob. "Condomania in Chicago." *Forbes,* November 1978.

"Time-Sharing: New Way to Buy a Vacation Home." *Changing Times,* January 1078.

Tymon, Dorothy. "Condominium Con Game." *McCalls,* October 1974.

"Why Apartments Are in Short Supply." *Business Week,* March 6, 1978.

NEWSPAPERS

"Aim Is Putting Nesters Back into the House." (New Haven) *Journal-Courier,* October 20, 1978.

Blumenthal, Ralph. "Guide for the Co-op Shopper." *New York Times,* March 4, 1979.

Brooks, Andree. "Condominium Sales Are Booming." *New York Times,* August 6, 1978.

———. "For the First-Home Buyer, Insecurity." *New York Times,* November 12, 1978.

———. "A House Divided: Condominiums in a Mansion." *New York Times,* February 15, 1979.

———. "Out of the Past, Two-Family Houses Are Coming Back." *New York Times,* February 25, 1979.

———. "Problems with the Condominium Boom." *New York Times,* January 28, 1979.

Brown, Betsy. "Life in Townhouse Condos: A Blend of Many Flavors."

New York Times, December 10, 1978.

Burzynski, Sue. "Condominium Shopping? Learn the Facts." (Lansing, Mich.) *State Journal,* February 21, 1977.

Carberry, James. "For Homeowners and Real-Estate Investors, Tax Law Offers a Variety of New Incentives." *Wall Street Journal,* February 12, 1979.

"Carey Signs Bill to Protect Tenants in Apartment-Building Converstion." *New York Times,* July 28, 1978.

"Condos Have Future Role." (New Haven) *Journal-Courier,* October 20, 1978.

"Condominium Concept to Spread." (Chicago) *Daily Defender,* November 21, 1978.

"Condo Owners Hold Election Wednesday." (Stamford, Conn.) *Advocate,* December 12, 1978.

Connolly, William G. "The Decision to Buy or Not to Buy." *New York Times,* January 21, 1979.

———. "Condominium Form Spreading in the City." *New York Times,* June 16, 1974.

———. "Condominium Proposals Fought." *New York Times,* April 21, 1974.

———. "Is a Custom Home Best? Or One in a Development?" *New York Times,* February 11, 1979.

———. "Should You Buy a New or an Old Home?" *New York Times,* February 4, 1979.

———. "Styles and Stories: Finding the Right Home Design." *New York Times,* January 28, 1979.

Cook, Louise. "Condominium Seen as Likely Home of Future." (Stamford, Conn.) *Advocate,* October 5, 1978.

Cunniff, John. "Housing Sales Soar in Spite of Rising Inflation." (Stamford, Conn.) *Advocate,* January 17, 1979.

Dreyfuss, Wayne. "Tranquility of California Village Tied to Its Planned Environment." (Stamford, Conn.) *Advocate,* February 16, 1979.

Edwards, Robert. "Shifting to a Condo? Why Not Rent Out Your House?" *Christian Science Monitor,* January 5, 1979.

Flicks, Robert B. "Condo Market Is Blossoming." *Hartford Courant,* October 18, 1978.

"Financing for Condo Is a First." (Memphis, Tenn.) *Commercial Appeal,* November 12, 1978.

Geniesse, Jane. "Squash Court, Sweet Squash Court." *New York Times,* November 16, 1978.

Goldberger, Paul. "Design Notebook." *New York Times,* March 8, 1979.

Henderson, Dan. "The City-State Survives." (Memphis, Tenn.) *Commercial Appeal,* April 9, 1978.

Hill, Susan. "Experts Offer Tips on Condominium Buying." (Stamford, Conn.) *Advocate,* November 14, 1978.

Hinds, Michael deCourcy. "At Your Service: Finding a Woodcarver." *New York Times,* July 27, 1978.

"Home Buyers Don't Wait." *Christian Science Monitor,* November 7, 1978.

Horsley, Carter B. "Cashing in on Co-op Fever: It Calls for Nerve and Timing." *New York Times,* December 3, 1978.

———. "For Homeowners, A Tax Windfall." *New York Times,* November 19, 1978.

"HUD Discloses Condominium Problems: Report to Fuel Bid for U.S. Rules on Sales." *Wall Street Journal,* August 22, 1975.

"HUD Moves to Avert Condo Resale Crisis." *Washington Star,* January 21, 1977.

Jindra, Christine J. "Condominiums Shun Renters: 'Kiss of Death.' " (Cleveland, Ohio) *Plain Dealer,* November 6, 1978.

Jones, Clayton. "Mobile Homes: Winning Acceptance." *Christian Science Monitor,* December 22, 1978.

Kaiser, Charles. "Co-ops: After the Boom, Stagnation, Uncertainty." *New York Times,* January 4, 1976.

Kaplan, Sam. "Westlake Lifestyle Thrives, Emphasizing Virtues of Affluent Suburbia." (Stamford, Conn.) *Advocate,* February 16, 1979.

Knickerbocker, Brad. "US Opens Home-Buying to a New Generation." *Christian Science Monitor,* November 9, 1978.

Koshar, John Leo. "Condominium Kills Resale Clause, Gets VA Loan OK." (Cleveland, Ohio) *Plain Dealer,* January 26, 1977.

Markham, Wayne. "New Rules for Condo Owners Become Law." *Miami* (Fla.) *Herald,* January 2, 1977.

———. "Will U.S. Law Kill Rec Leases?" *Miami* (Fla.) *Herald,* April 30, 1978.

——— and Eiland, Darrell. "Condo Owners Saving Millions by Buying Recreation Leases." *Miami* (Fla.) *Herald,* January 24, 1977.

Miller, Stephen B. "Trespass, Vandalism, the Police and Condominium Schizophrenia." (Stamford, Conn.) *Advocate,* December 2, 1978.

"National Law Group Tackles Condo Code." (Honolulu) *Bulletin & Advertiser,* July 24, 1977.

'New Starts and Conversions May Equal Record This Year." (Boston) *Herald American,* January 15, 1978.

Obermark, Jerome. "Condo Owners Beset by Mountain Upkeep Expenses." (Memphis, Tenn.) *Commercial Appeal,* November 19, 1978.

Oser, Alan S. "About Real Estate." *New York Times,* February 2, 1979.

———. "Condominiums Near the Heart of a Town." *New York Times,* February 9, 1979.

———. "Housing—It shelters More Than the Family." *New York Times,* January 28, 1979.

Parry, Bill. "Condos: Housing Concept of Future—and the Past." *San Diego* (Calif.) *Union,* April 23, 1978.

Pasztor, Andy. "Court OKs Rec-Lease Collections." *Miami* (Fla.) *Herald,* April 13, 1978.

Phalon, Richard. "Family Money: the Pitfalls in Budgeting for a Condominium." *New York Times,* November 24, 1977.

Porter, Sylvia. "Home Sale After 55; $100,000 Tax-Free." *New York Daily News,* February 27, 1979.

Rejnis, Ruth. "Caution Is Urged for Condominium Buyers." *New York Times,* June 4, 1978.

———. "Condominiums: 'An Adventure.' " *New York Times,* May 28, 1978.

Rugaber, Walter. "Few States Protect Condominium Buyers." *New York Times,* June 16, 1974.

Schreiber, Jody. "Nation's Craving for Condominiums Hits Home in Tucson." (Tucson) *Arizona Daily Star,* August 21, 1977.

Schuman, Wendy. "Co-op Owners Battle Rise in Costs." *New York Times,* January 11, 1979.

Shaman, Diana. "Simple 'For Sale' Signs Are Not So Simple." *New York Times,* December 31, 1978.

Skurka, Norma. "Ski Homes." *New York Times,* December 16, 1976.

Sloane Leonard. "Personal Finance: Condominium Rules and Rights." *New York Times,* January 23, 1975.

Stanford, Gregory D. "Co-op Form of Housing Gets a Boost." *Milwaukee* (Wisc.) *Journal,* November 12, 1978.

Teasley, Colleen. "Atlanta Condo Market Emerges from Doldrums." *Atlanta* (Ga.) *Journal,* April 9, 1978.

Volsky, George. "Floridians Buying Condominiums." *New York Times,* October 22, 1972.

Wedemeyer, Dee. "Developer Finding Co-ops Are Still in Great Demand." *New York Times,* July 28, 1978.

Woodward, James M. "Condo on Road to Revival." *Hartford Courant,* October 15, 1978.

————. "Pressure Mounts for Resale Home Warranties." *Christian Science Monitor,* December 22, 1978.

BOOKS

Berman, Daniel S. *How to Organize and Sell a Profitable Real Estate Condominium.* Englewood Cliffs, N.J.: Prentice-Hall, 1966.

Brooks, Patricia, and Brooks, Lester. *How to Buy a Condominium.* New York: Stein and Day, 1975.

Butcher, Les. *The Condominium Book.* Princeton, N.J.: Princeton University Press, 1975.

Clurman, David. *Cooperatives and Condominiums.* New York: John Wiley and Sons, 1970.

Cobleigh, Ira U. *About Credit.* Washington, D.C.: U.S. News & World Report Books, 1975.

Condominium Buyers' Guide. Washington, D.C.: National Association of Home Builders, n.d.

Gray, Genevieve. *Condominiums: How to Buy, Sell and Live in Them.* New York: Funk and Wagnalls, 1975.

How to Buy Real Estate. London: Collier Books, 1970.

Hubin, Vincent J. *Warning!* Chicago, Ill.: Dow Jones-Irwin, 1976.

Karr, James N. *The Condominium Buyer's Guide.* New York: Frederick Fell, 1973.

Kehoe, Patrick E. *Cooperatives and Condominiums.* Dobbs Ferry, N.Y.: Oceana Publications, 1974.

Managing a Successful Community Association. Washington, D.C.: Urban Land Institute, n.d.

Norcross, Carl. *Townhouses and Condominiums: Residents' Likes and Dislikes.* Washington, D.C.: The Urban Land Institute, 1973.

Reskin, Melvin A. and Sakai, Hiroshi. *Modern Condominium Forms.* Boston, Mass.: Warren Publ., 1971.

Questions About Condominiums. Washington, D.C.: Department of Housing and Urban Development, 1977.

Romney, Keith B. *Condominium Development Guide.* Boston, Mass.: Warren Publ., 1974.

Rosen, Lawrence R. *The Dow Jones-Irwin Guide to Interest.* Homewood, Ill.: Dow Jones-Irwin, 1974.

Rothenberg, Henry H. *What You Should Know About Condominiums.* Radnor, Pa.: Chilton Books, 1974.

Thompson, Elizabeth Kendall, Ed. *Apartments, Townhouses and Condominiums.* New York: McGraw-Hill, 1975.

To the Home-Buying Veteran. Washington, D.C.: Veterans Administration, 1977.

Index

Administration, 111
Advantages, 3, 9, 11, 50–2, 117–22,
  126–7
Advisory committee, 135–6
Agenda, association meeting, 152, 154
Air-conditioning, 139–40, 141
"Air space estate," 5
Albany (New York), 29
Alps, 43, 44
Amortization, 56
Amortized mortgage, 87–8
Annual expenses, 44
Apartment
  conversion of, 25, 26, 31, 54–6,
    124–5, 165–7
  cooperative, 11–2
  high-rise, 4, 5, 11, 18
  ownership apartment, 29
  rental, 49–50
  Roman, 16
Appraisal fee, 100–1
Assessments
  authority to assess, 107
  flood control, 143
  maintenance, 7, 109
  operation of common property, 7
  payment of, 127
  projected, 75–6
  reserve, 109
  sewer, 143
  special, 59–60, 112, 143
  uncollected, 57, 60, 107
  underestimated, 74
  undivided real estate, 7
Atlanta (Georgia), 32
Attorney, 102, 104, 116, 138
  fees of, 100, 116

Babylonian document, 16
Balloon mortgage, 97–8
Beverly Hills (California), 33
Board of directors, association, 8, 59,
    135–6, 153–4
  actions in hiring manager, 138
  builder as director, 136
  chairman of, 156–7
  establishment by enabling declara-
    tion, 106
  meetings of, 154
  of cooperative, 11, 12, 57
  officers, 155–6
  of PUD, 13
  preempted powers of, 81
  president of, 156–8
  responsibilities of, 112, 154–5
  "straw board," 81–3
Boston (Massachusetts), 32
Boundaries
  artificial, 4
  natural, 4
  of apartment, 5
  of condominium, 5, 6, 23
  of total property, 7
Brooklyn (New York) Museum, 16
Budget committee, 153
Budget, operating, 74, 112
  See also Maintenance budget
Builder (see Developer)
Bylaws, association, 7, 59, 79, 80–1,
    102, 104, 111–3
  amending of, 112, 113
  checklist for, 112–3
  cooperative, 12, 57
  enforcing compliance with, 113
  general provisions of, 112–3

owner's responsibilities and rights, 111–2
renting provisions of, 146
settling disputes, 113
tenure of office clause, 154

California, 22, 30, 117
Canada, 45
Capital gains, 10, 45
  tax on, 52–4
  See also Revenue Act of 1978
Caribbean Islands, 45
Casualty coverage, 76
Checklists
  for bylaws, 113–4
  for condominium buyers, 61–72
  for condominium documents, 116
  for enabling declaration, 107–11
  for purchase and sales contract, 104–6
Chicago (Illinois), 19, 30, 31, 55–6
Children, 37, 44, 68, 75, 115
City-state, Greek, 14
Closing costs, 99–101
Cluster housing units, 37–8
  resort, 43
Collateral, 45, 86
  use of condominium unit as, 109
Colonial America, 14, 17
Commercial office space, 34, 46–8
  advantages of 47–8
  industrial park, 47
Committee
  advisory, 135–6
  budget, 153
  grounds, 152
  swimming pool, 152
  tennis, 153
Committees, homeowners association, 152
Common area, 5–6
  See also Common property
Common elements, 6
  See also Common property
Common estate, 6
  See also Common property
Common facilities, 143
Common green, 37
Common property, 6, 8, 40, 41, 56, 77, 112, 113

in PUD, 13
operation of, 7
owner's percentage in, 7
Common space, 5–6
Commons, 17
Communality, 15
Communal living, 17, 128, 164–5
Condo (See Condominium)
Condominium
  buyer's advice on, 73–84
  comparison with cooperative, 56–8
  comparison with rented apartment, 49–50
  comparison with single-family house, 58–9, 119, 162–3
  deed to, 8
  design of, 61–2
  definition of, 3
  future of, 159–69
  location of, 63–4
  obligations of ownership, 59–60
  shopping for, 49–60
  types of, 34–48
  unit ratios in, 110
  used as collateral, 45, 86, 109
Condominium communities, 41
Condominium unit, 6
  average price of (1978), 58
  comparison with single-family home, 58–9
  description of enabling declaration, 7–8, 14
Construction, condominium, 20, 68–70, 78, 92, 125–6
Controlled communality, 12–3
Conversion of condominium, 25, 26
  advantage to renter, 55–6
  Chicago regulations, 31
  duplex, 168–9
  in reverse, 146
  New York State law, 29–30
  San Francisco regulations, 31
  split, 124–5
  town house, 38
  what to do about, 54–6, 165–7
Cooling-off period (waiting period), 80, 104
Co-op (See Cooperative)
Cooperative, 10, 11–12
  board of directors of, 57–8

compared to condominium, 56–8
financing of, 57
New York conversion law (July 27, 1978), 29–30
proprietary lease, 57
selling restriction, 58
Corporate ownership
cooperative shares, 10, 11, 56–7
PUD, 13
Country estate condominium, 37, 40–1, 122
"Country town house," 38–9
Covenants (See Restrictions)
Credit report, 100
Cubes of space, 5–6

Dallas (Texas), 32
Deed, 8, 106, 116
Density (of housing), 123
Denver (Colorado), 32
Department of Housing and Urban Development (HUD), 19, 25–6
Deposit, 103–5
See also Non-binding reservation
Depreciation deduction, 48
Design, architectural, 122
Designated lender, 83
Developer, 13, 20, 21, 24, 27, 35
abuses of, 27, 73–84
as manager, 135–6
establishing association, 135
leadership training, 134–5
Directors, board of (See Board of Directors)
Disadvantages, 3, 122–7
District of Columbia (See Washington, D.C.)
Document, 7, 102–16
See also Bylaws and House rules, Enabling declaration, Purchase agreement,
Down payment, 104, 105
abuses relating to, 77–8
Duplex, 34, 37, 39
conversion of, 167–9
rental of, 38

"Earnest money," 103–4
Elections (in homeowners association), 111, 155

Elevator, 69, 114, 115
maintenance of, 141, 142
Enabling declaration, 7–8, 13, 79–80, 102, 104, 106–7
checklist for, 107–11
Energy crisis, 163
Equity, 9, 51–2, 88, 119
Escalating clause, 23
Escrow, 77–8, 91, 101, 104
Estate
common, 8
country, 37, 40–1
single deed, 8
space, 76
Evanston (Illinois), 31–32
Exchange network, 45
Exclusion right, 54
Exclusive use clause, 3
"Express warranty," 83

Facilities, 68–9
See also Recreational facilities
Federal Housing Administration (FHA), 18, 101
loans, 75, 77, 89–94
prepayment clause in, 99, 101
Federal Trade Commission (FTC), 26
Fee
accountant's, 137
appraisal, 100–1
attorney's, 100, 116
facilities, 22
lender's origination, 100
maintenance, 12, 26, 46, 47, 55, 106, 108, 136, 137, 141, 150
management, 20
Fee simple ownership, 75
FHA (See Federal Housing Administration)
Financing of condominium, 85–101
Financing of resort condominium, 45
First refusal clause, 58, 75, 93
Fixed costs, 137, 142
Flood control assessments, 143
Florida, 19, 20, 21, 22, 23, 26, 30, 44
Fort Lauderdale (Florida), 31, 32
Fort Worth (Texas), 32
Fourplex, 37, 38, 39, 40
France, 17

Garbage disposal, 69, 140
Garden apartments, 34, 37
Georgia, 26
Graduated-payment mortgage, 89, 98
Grounds, 8, 9, 140, 141–2, 152

Hawaii, 18, 26, 44
Health care, 41
Heating system, 139, 140, 141
High-rise, 4, 5, 9, 11, 18, 21, 34, 35, 37,
  39, 43, 69, 117, 123, 124–5
Homeowners association, 7, 14, 113,
  125, 127, 148–58
  as mini-government, 148
  board of directors of, 153–4
  bylaws of, 110–4
  committees of, 152–3
  creation of, 134–6
  management responsibilities of,
    136–47
  meetings of, 150–2
  membership in, 148–50
  of cooperative, 12
  officers of, 155–6
  of PUD, 13, 84
  president of, 156–8
  voting rules of, 7, 109, 112, 150–1
Horizontal property, 17, 18
Horizontal Property Regimes Act, 18
Hotel clause (See Transient clause)
House rules, 102, 104, 114–5, 125, 135
  example of, 114–5
Housing units, 11
Houston (Texas), 30, 32
HUD (See Department of Housing
  and Urban Development)

"Implied warranty," 83
Income tax, 9, 36, 48, 50–4, 56, 139
Industrial park, 47
Inflation, 28, 36, 52, 88
  hedge against, 45, 119, 168
Inside space, 3, 5
Insurance, 112, 113
  casualty, 76, 77
  casualty, hazard and liability, 77
  fire, 101
  hazard and liability, 7, 77, 107
  liability, 59, 76–7, 79

  premiums on, 142
  title, 16, 100
Interest, 50, 51, 87, 88
Internal Revenue Service (See In-
  come tax)
Interval ownership, 43
Investment, condominium as, 9,
  119–20

Janitor service, 140
Juvenal, 121

Land record office, 4
"Land rent" charge, 21
Landscaping, 62
Latin America, 17
Laundry facility, 69
Lawyer (See Attorney)
Lease, 57
Lease-back clause, 92
  See also Leasehold clause and Re-
    creational lease
Leasehold clause, 73–4
  See also Recreational lease and
    Lease-back clause
Leasehold condominium, 110
  See also Lease-back clause, Lease-
    hold clause and Recreational
    lease
Legislation, condominium, 17, 26–7,
  29
Lender's orgigination fee, 100
Lien, property, 59, 107, 112
Lifestyle in condominium, 13, 15, 35,
  117–31, 159–65
Loans, 7, 18
  amortized, 87–8
  auto, 86–7
  conventional, 90, 94
  FHA, 89–93
  mortgage, 85–101
  personal, 57
  VA, 53, 89–93
  See also Mortgage
Location of condominium, 63–4
Location of condominium unit, 67
Los Angeles (California), 30, 32
"Lowballing," 74
Low-rise, 35, 37

Maintenance, 9, 40, 58, 59, 92, 113, 125
  budget for, 20, 74, 138, 144
  costs of, 57, 140–2
  equipment for, 141
  fees for, 12, 26, 46, 47, 55, 74, 75, 106, 107, 108, 136, 137, 141
  freedom from, 9, 42, 50, 118–9
  of PUD, 13
Management, 125
  contract for, 21, 22, 24, 80, 116, 147
  costs of, 137–9
  fee for, 20, 47, 137
  professional, 7, 112
  responsibility of, 144–5
  staff for, 138–9
Management company, 80, 81
Management contract, 21, 22, 24, 116
  non-cancellable, 80, 147
Manager, 8, 12, 132, 137, 157–8
  as employee of board of directors, 136
  builder as, 81, 134, 136
  relationship with builder, 150
  relationship with president of association, 157–8
Mansion unit, 37, 39–40, 122
Maryland, 26
Massachusetts, 26
Master deed, 106
Mediterranean, 43, 44
Miami (Florida), 18, 19, 31, 32
Michigan, 19
Middle Ages, 17
Mid-rise, 35, 37
Monthly charges, 112
  default in, 57, 107
Mortgage, 9, 10, 12
  amortized, 87–8
  assumption of existing mortgage, 95–7
  balloon, 97–8
  bank conditions for, 95
  closing costs of, 99–101
  conventional, 90, 94
  FHA, 89–93
  financing of, 85
  graduated-payment, 89, 98

  interest deductions for, 50
  interest on unpaid balance of, 87
  kinds of, 89–94
  loan for, 102
  open-end clause in, 99
  payments of, 105
  points in, 98
  prepayment clause in, 99
  processing charge for, 100–1
  second, 97–8
  VA, 53, 89–93
Mortgage interest rate, 88

Nassau County (New York), 29
National Housing Act, 18
Netherlands, The, 17
New York City, 19, 32, 56
New York (State), 26
  conversion law in, 29
Nonbinding reservation, 102, 103, 105
North Miami Beach (Florida), 24

Oakland (California), 33
"$100,000 Tax-free Home Sale," 52–4
Open-end mortgage, 99
Operating reserve, 7, 137
Operational costs, 137, 139–40
Outside space, 3, 5–6
Overcrowding, 122–4
Ownership apartment, 29
  See also Conversion
Ownership
  alternatives to home ownership, 10
  common, 5, 6
  condominium, 8
  fee simple, 75
  interval, 43
  joint, 3
  obligations of, 59–60
  of street-level stores, 35
  percentage of, 7, 108
  plan of, 106
  private, 2
  responsibilities of, 111
  split, 3
  undivided, 3, 5, 6, 8
  vacation, 43
  villa-share, 43

See also Time-sharing and Corporate ownership

Parking, 3, 21, 41, 47, 62, 72, 107, 115, 123
Participatory democracy, 14
Percentage of ownership, 7, 75–6
Pets, 75, 114, 115, 124
Planned unit development (PUD), 12–3, 84
Points, 98
Prepayment clause in mortgage, 99
President of association, 156–8
  relationship to condominium manager, 157–8
Privacy, 123–4
Processing charge for mortgage, 100–1
Property, 3, 4, 5
  common, 5, 6, 8, 107
  horizontal, 17, 18
  legal description of, 6
  value of, 64–6
Proprietary lease, 57
Proxy, 112
Public transportation, 163
PUD (See Planned unit development)
Puerto Rico, 17, 18, 44
Purchase and sales agreement (sales contract) 79–80, 102–6

Quorum, 112

Real estate, 3, 8
  assessment of, 7, 109
  tax on, 9, 56, 100–1, 106
  See also Tax deduction
Reciprocal-use agencies, 45
Recording fee, 100
Recreational facilities, 3, 10, 22, 23, 24, 41, 43, 44, 46, 75, 78–9, 108, 115, 121
  checklist for, 68–70
  fee for, 22
Recreational lease, 22, 24, 73–4
  See also Lease-back clause and Leasehold clause
Rentals, 10, 28
  apartment, 49–50, 57

comparison with condominium ownership, 49–50
conversions of, 26, 29, 54–6, 124–5, 165–7
duplex, 38
resort, 46
unsold units of, 22, 105, 124–5, 146
Repairs, 21, 42, 60, 113, 143
Resale of resort condominium, 45
Resale restrictions, 58, 75
Resale value, 48, 67–8
Reserve fund, 7, 137, 143–4
Residential unit, 34, 46
Resort condominium, 34, 42–6
  advantages of, 44–6
  annual expenses of, 44
  financing of, 45
  investment in, 46
  resale of, 45
Restrictions (covenants), 111, 112
  declaration of, 106
  long-term, 80
  on partitioning units, 110
  on resale, 58, 75
Revenue Act of 1978, 52–4
Robert's Rules of Order, 157
Rockland County (New York), 29
Roman Empire, 16
Row house (See Town house)
Rules and regulations (See House rules)

Sales contract (See Purchase and sales agreement)
Salesmanship
  dishonest, 126
  high-pressure, 79–80
San Diego (California), 30, 33
San Francisco (California), 31, 33
San Juan (Puerto Rico), 17, 18
Santa Monica (California), 55
Seattle (Washington), 33
Second mortgage, 97–8
Security (See Collateral)
Security measures, 42, 69, 121–2, 125, 140
Settlement of disputes, 113
Sewer assessments, 143

Single-family house
  average price of (1978), 58
  comparison with condominium, 58–9, 119, 162–3
  high cost of, 162–3, 168
Snow removal, 140
Social-Security withholding, 137, 139
Spain, 17, 45
Special assessments, 59, 112, 143
State laws, 112
  See also Legislation
Street-level shops, 47
  ownership of, 35
Substitute unit, 78
Suburban condominium, 34, 37–42
Surety bond, 92
Survey, property, 100
Swimming pool, 10, 21, 24, 41, 59, 62, 67, 70, 74, 121, 139, 140, 141
  committee for, 152–3

Tax deduction, income, 9, 36, 50, 51, 56, 67, 87–8, 120
  in commercial condominium, 48
Tax, real estate, 9, 56, 100, 101, 106, 107
Tax shelter, 36, 47
Tennis court, 10, 21, 41, 67, 70, 121, 153
Time-interval ownership (See Time sharing)
Time sharing, 43–6, 53
Title, 91
Title insurance, 16, 100
Title search, 100
Town house, 34, 37, 38–9, 117
Town meetings, 14
Transfer taxes, 100
Transient clause, 92

Transient occupancy, 76, 92
Triplex, 38, 39

Uncollected assessments, 60
Undivided interest, 3, 5, 6, 7, 8, 13, 38, 39, 41, 84, 92
  in commercial condominium, 46
  in industrial park, 47
Undivided ownership (See Undivided interest)
Unit description, 103
United States, 17, 18, 19, 27
Unit estate, 6
Unit substitution, 78
Unsold units, 22, 105, 125, 146
Urban condominium, 34, 35–7
Urban Land Institute, 117, 118, 149
Utilities, 139

VA (See Veterans Administration)
Vacation condominium (See Resort condominium)
Veterans Administration (VA) loan, 53, 89–94, 99
Villa shares, 43
Virginia, 26

Waiting period (See Cooling-off period)
Warranty, 26, 110, 116
  "express," 83
  "implied," 83
Washington (state), 44
Washington, D.C., 26, 29, 30, 31, 32
Water, 139
Westchester County (New York), 29

Zoning laws, 66–7, 110